Creative Flower Arranging

This Book Belongs to

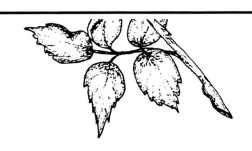

Creative Flower Arranging
FLORAL DESIGN
FOR HOME AND FLOWER SHOW

by
Betty Belcher

Photographs by Richard Moore
Illustrations by Denise Hoage

TIMBER PRESS
Portland, Oregon

For permission to reproduce works from the following collections, grateful acknowledgment is hereby made to

Philadelphia Museum of Art, A. E. Gallatin Collection, "Le Courrier" by Georges Braque.

Whitney Museum of American Art, "Sea Scape" by Alexander Calder.

Appreciation is also extended to National Council of State Garden Clubs, Inc., for permission to reprint their color wheel.

All photographs are by
Richard Moore

Designs by Deen Day Smith appear on pages 22, 160, and 180; designs by Hallie Brown appear on pages 125 and 143; and a design by Martha Allen appears on page 83. All other designs are by the author.

Reprinted 1994, 1995

ISBN 0-88192-229-3 (hardback)
ISBN 0-88192-247-1 (paperback)
Printed in Hong Kong

TIMBER PRESS, INC.
The Haseltine Building
133 S.W. Second Avenue, Suite 450
Portland, Oregon 97204-3527

Library of Congress Cataloging-in-Publication Data

Belcher, Betty.
    Creative flower arranging : floral design for home and flower show
/ by Betty Belcher ; photographs by Richard Moore ; illustrations by
Denise Hoage.
        p.   cm.
    Includes bibliographical references (p.   ) and index.
    ISBN 0-88192-229-3 (hardback)
    ISBN 0-88192-247-1 (paperback)
    1. Flower arrangement.   I. Title.
SB449.B374   1993
745.92--dc20   92-41061
                                                                    CIP

Table of Contents

Dedication

To Abner, whose patience and love have made this possible; to daughters Cathie, Deanna, Denise, and Cheryl and their families for their support and understanding; and to the National Council of State Garden Clubs, whose Flower Show Schools program changed my life.

Foreword

As floral artists approach the year 2000, the challenge is greater to create designs that express the changing lifestyles and challenges of our era. All art works, including floral art, reflect the period of time during which the artist worked. The exploration of space, for example, has introduced space within our designs, leading to new and innovative arrangements and staging. As in other works, computerization, rapid transit systems, and instant communication will continue to inspire floral designers and freshly influence our ideas and art.

Before creating a floral design, we must first understand the many facets of flower arranging—from containers and mechanics, to selecting and conditioning plant material, to the inspiration to create the final design. Not only have these subjects been covered in detail in this informative book, but other topics are explored as well: beginning designs, history of floral design in art, Creative designs, and staging, among others. Illustrations and color photographs created by the author provide the reader with both instruction and inspiration.

The artist-author served the National Council of State Garden Clubs on the Flower Show Schools Committee and was the committee's chairman for over six years, during which time she led the revision of the *Handbook for Flower Shows*. This well qualifies Mrs. Belcher to write this treatise on floral art design, from its beginning to the present day. It provides a complete overview of our past, documents the present, and provides a springboard into the future.

Mrs. Lofton M. Milstead, Jr.
Chairman
NCSGC Flower Show Schools Committee
July 1992

Preface

Flower arranging is now widely recognized as an art form, but little mention is made of this stature in recent, albeit beautifully produced, books on floral design. Rather, the art-conscious beginner must scour a wide variety of sources—often reading between the lines for the particular focus sought—for information of the most basic kind on the history of flower arranging and the elements and principles of design. Actual "how-to" instructions for simple designs are practically nonexistent. Worst of all, little or nothing has been offered the serious student of floral design on the subject of preparation of arrangements for flower shows, a much-enjoyed facet of the flower arranging experience for many.

A handful of excellent flower arranging books—published in the 1960s and '70s—are now out of print, and naturally do not include current styles, though they are well worth the search as additional study tools if they can be located.

Such is the yawning gap this book seeks to fill. It speaks to both the beginning arranger and the experienced designer, offering in clear, simple language the information and guidance needed, whether the reader's desire is to arrange flowers for use in the home, flower show, place of worship, or other venue. The arrangements considered, the illustrations, the photos—all have been kept as pure and exemplary as possible and are described in terms compatible with the 1987 edition of the *Handbook for Flower Shows* of the National Council of State Garden Clubs.

Design styles—Traditional and Creative—will come and go and come again; no art form remains static. After presenting the necessary grounding in Traditional designs—their debt to times past, their recent history, and actual hands-on construction—this book will focus on the newer Creative designs, which better allow for, encourage, and even celebrate the evolution of floral design. If it helps flower arrangers better understand their art and develop their own individual creativity, my goals will have been met.

Betty Belcher
September 1992

Acknowledgments

It is difficult to thank all those individuals who have had a part in an endeavor such as this, for even our childhood experiences continue to have a bearing on current accomplishments, great and small. One of my earliest memories was as momentous as it is pleasant to recall: I visited the garden of a lovely woman—who years later became my mother-in-law—and was given a bouquet of beautiful flowers to take home. Both the garden and the keepsake remembrance made a lasting impression on me and were perhaps the beginning of a life-long love of gardening and flower arranging.

That memorable bouquet was but a glimpse of this new world. As a new bride, I found that membership in the local garden club opened wide the door. As the years passed, I became happily involved in all aspects of gardening and particularly in flower arranging. My family was unflaggingly supportive, often bringing home found objects they thought I might like to use in a design, never once complaining when the refrigerator and the bathtub were full of plant material for a flower show. To all my family, my deepest love and gratitude. You are the best!

Others to whom gratitude is due: certain garden club friends who urged me to write this book—you know who you are!; Junne Johnsrud, who first appointed me the chairman of the National Council Flower Show Schools—surely the most rewarding and time-consuming chairmanship ever; Deen Day Smith, for her boundless encouragement; Richard Moore, photographer extraordinaire, for his patience during the process and the superb quality of the results; Ann Milstead and Hallie Brown, for reviewing the text; Denise Hoage, for her beautiful line drawings; and Cheryl Eberle, for help in proofreading and her faithful service as a sounding board.

Special thanks to Richard Abel, whose interest in such a book resulted in my serious commitment to the project, and to my delightful editor, Frances Farrell, whose ability to rephrase and punctuate have been invaluable. Lastly, to all those designers whose programs, classes, or books have been an inspiration—thank you!

1 A Brief History of Floral Design

Almost everyone, as a child, picked a fistful of dandelions or buttercups and carried them home to a delighted mother who swiftly placed this precious and loving gift in water to keep it—and the thought that accompanied it—fresh as long as possible. This may have been our first lesson about the keeping quality of flowers.

As we grew older, flowers played increasingly important roles in our lives. Many grew up with the charming custom of making a May basket and filling it with flowers to be left surreptitiously on someone's doorstep. There were flowers on Valentine's Day and birthdays; a corsage for the prom; roses at graduation; a special wedding bouquet; an orchid on Mother's Day. Seasonally, one looks forward to seeing the first purple crocus of spring or a pot of white lilies at Easter. Along with mums and marigolds, we arrange gourds, dried corn, and crisp apples in the harvest cornucopia. Poinsettias, wreaths of holly, and swags of laurel mean the holiday season has finally arrived.

Blooming plants from our own gardens don't always completely satisfy our celebratory, decorative, or aesthetic needs, and so to augment them, we occasionally purchase cut flowers from the local florist or supermarket. Inevitably, there is an urge to arrange all these beautiful blooms in a more pleasing manner, and we are launched into the wonderful world of flower arranging.

We may be content to arrange a few flowers for the dining table, the living room, or hall, or we may become so consumed by this love of flowers and expression of our creativity that exhibiting in a flower show is the next step. In any event, the goals are similar and the rewards sweet.

A basic knowledge of its history provides the necessary foundation for floral design, whether for home or flower show. To understand even a little about how flowers influenced our forebears adds interest to our hobby and serves as a link with the past. The information offered here has been gleaned from museum collections, art history references, and the many available books on the history of floral design in Europe and the Orient. There is much to learn!

INTERNATIONAL STIRRINGS

Plants have played a vital role in human experience since Eve gave the apple to Adam. They were necessary for food, medicinal purposes, and shelter. No one knows for sure when flowers were first offered as a token of love, sympathy, or respect, or brought indoors to be enjoyed solely for their beauty, but such nonessential early uses are well documented.

All art forms, including floral design, flourished during times of peace and prosperity. When wars erupted or times were otherwise difficult, art forms diminished or disappeared. As civilization progressed and life became easier, flowers took up what we consider to be their accustomed role in daily life. Much information about the early use of flowers in such a purely decorative capacity is still with us in the artifacts of various civilizations.

Archeologists and art historians agree that the use of cut flowers in water-filled containers dates back for many centuries. A visit to any art museum or gallery offers much in support of this notion and will attest to the importance of floral design through history. Indications are that floral arrangements were limited to religious ceremonies at first. As far back as 2500 BC, the Egyptians were using plant material for this and other decorative purposes as shown by the carved reliefs and painted wall decorations unearthed by archeologists. Flowers were cut and placed in vases of glass or terra cotta. Many of these had several spouts to hold individual blooms; the same style of vase was later used in both Persia and Holland. Designs were highly stylized and apparently rules were strict as there were few variations for centuries. Lotus (thought to be a sacred blossom), herbs, palm, and papyrus were often used, as were blue scillas, Siberian iris, anemones, and tazetta narcissus.

Throughout the Classical Greek and Roman periods, flowers were used in very similar ways, though flowers and foliage were often liberated from vases. Wreaths and garlands were wound around pillars, carried on staves, or worn by athletes, civic leaders, and other important individuals as a mark of distinction. Rose petals were strewn on floors, streets, lakes, and tables during the time of Nero and Cleopatra. For the beautification of their lavish banquets, the Romans developed a means of forcing roses indoors by using hot water pipes.

In medieval times, many useful plants were tended by monks within monastery walls. Wars and continued unrest allowed little time for cultivating plants other than those grown for food or medicinal purposes. Church altars were sometimes decorated with plant materials; however, few flowers were grown for their beauty alone.

Chinese artifacts reveal that cut flowers placed in water-filled containers were used on the altars of temples during the T'ang dynasty (618–906 AD). Paintings on silks, scrolls, and vases; embroidery; and ivory, bronze, and wood carvings from this period all demonstrate this early use of plant material.

The Chinese had a great love and appreciation of flowers and foliage. Their Buddhist training instilled in them a high regard for all life, therefore they cut plant material very sparingly. Designs used a minimum of cut flowers in a natural manner. The exception was the large amounts of plant material required in their basket designs.

Plant material had a symbolic meaning for the Chinese as well, which played an important part in the development of their floral designs. For example, the

pear, peach, and bamboo symbolized long life; white plum blossoms repre-
sented winter; peach and cherry blossoms meant spring; the lotus depicted
summer; and chrysanthemums signified fall.

Buddhism was introduced into Japan around the middle of the 6th century
AD by monks who brought their flower-arranging skills with them as well as their
faith. Both were well accepted. The practice of offering flower arrangements to
Buddha was a traditional part of this religion; the floral offerings were fashioned
by the monks themselves. As time passed, the custom of employing floral
arrangements for solely religious purposes was relaxed. The nobility were the
first to use floral arrangements outside of the religious sphere, and later their use
by all Japanese regardless of class became commonplace. In the 16th century, the
upper class began holding flower-arranging contests.

Until very recently, every traditional Japanese house had at least one room
with a traditional tokonoma, a special alcove in which was displayed a grouping
of items. This grouping usually included a scroll painting or calligraphic inscrip-
tion, a treasured art object, and a flower arrangement. The tokonoma was the
focal point of the room which otherwise had few, if any, furnishings.

Ikebana (Japanese flower arranging) has long been considered an art form
in Japan; the oldest known book on flower arranging is Japanese, dating back to
1445. There are several schools of Japanese design, each with a headmaster. The
Ikenobo School was founded in the middle of the 15th century. Other schools
developed over the years, and both the Ohara and Sogetsu schools were founded
in the 20th century. Styles in these many schools range from the traditional to the
very creative.

Japanese floral designs are asymmetrical and most show typical Oriental
restraint in the amount of plant material used. The choice of plant material, line
directions, angles—all have subtle meanings. General simplicity and beauty of
line are the outstanding features, with great emphasis placed on the specific
proportions among the major lines. Japanese flower arrangements are never
judged, but merely enjoyed for their beauty. Oriental designs have had a great
influence on designs in the United States, as we shall see.

EUROPEAN DESIGNS

Meanwhile flower arranging was developing in Europe. Turkey and Persia
contributed the cone-shaped design during the Byzantine period (500–1453 AD).
These designs were tall, slender, and tapering, and the container was usually a
chalice or urn. Ribbon was often spiraled around a design of lilies, daisies, carnations, pine, grapes, and other fruits. Rich, jewel-toned colors were favored.

After the fall of the Roman Empire, there was a new interest in growing
flowers for their appearance rather than their utility. The great artists of the period
have left us a valuable legacy of paintings which beautifully document this trend.

In the early 17th century, European artists produced still-life masterpieces
with great masses of flowers in vases. Fruits, birds, insects, or animal skins and
carcasses were placed in the flower arrangement or on the table around it. These
early paintings show round or oval designs in containers which range from the
very ornate to classic urns and compotes. Many designs appear to have been
placed on pedestals, in niches, or sometimes out-of-doors. A few painters have
included two designs in a single painting, suggesting they were made to be used
together.

Carnations arranged in a cone shape reminiscent of the Byzantine period.

Flowers that did not normally bloom in the same season are often pictured together. Art historians feel these unnatural juxtapositions result from drawings made in different seasons, combined into a painting at a later date purely for their form or color. These designs all contain large masses of flowers and foliage which frequently nearly cover the container. Columbine, iris, lilies, lilies-of-the-valley, marigolds, pansies, pinks, and roses bloom in simultaneous profusion. One painting by Guido Cagnacci (Italian 1601–1663) shows flowers in an old wine flask whose raffia cover is beginning to unwrap. The raffia curling down the side of the flask, adding textural change and rhythm, has a creative appearance which would still be effective today.

While many of the early flower paintings show very full, overdone arrangements with a multitude of flowers, in the mid 18th century, by contrast, the French painter Jean-Baptiste Siméon Chardin painted "Flowers in a Porcelain Vase." This is a very simple design of red, white, and blue flowers in a blue and gray vase. The flowers are impressionistic forms rather than carefully rendered blooms. Shapes are recognizable as round or slightly elongated, giving the impression of roses, tuberoses, and baby's breath massed together in bouquet form.

By the mid to late 19th century, European artists began to develop a less compact style with flowers more carefully arranged. In a common pattern, the largest blooms were placed near the point of emergence from the container, with the smaller blooms at the top and outer edges. Grasses were also incorporated into the designs.

Containers ranged from earthenware jugs, glass tumblers, or simple vases to those of heavy Venetian glass, marble, or bronze. Often the container was almost completely hidden by a profusion of flowers, other plant material, and accessories. Flower colors were mixed or analogous, and the background was often very dark, creating a lustrous effect.

Historically, European floral designs fall into the following periods and styles.

Classical Greek and Roman

During the Classical Greek and Roman periods (600 BC–325 AD), plant material was most commonly used in the form of wreaths or garlands. Branches of boxwood, ivy, laurel, oak, or yew; herbs, such as parsley and bay leaves; or apples, grapes, figs and other fruits were often included. Flowers—such as honeysuckles, hyacinths, lilies, and roses—were selected for their scent. Artists record little use of cut flowers in water-filled containers. Simplicity and symmetry prevailed.

Italian Renaissance

In the Italian Renaissance (14th through 16th centuries), designs gave an impression of richness and grandeur, resulting from the use of warm, intense colors, often accented by cool colors. Containers of bronze, marble, or heavy Venetian glass held masses of dried flowers or tropical fruits with fresh flowers. Della Robbia wreaths, evidence of the Roman heritage, were also popular at this time.

Dutch and Flemish

Designs of the Dutch and Flemish periods (17th and 18th centuries) combined a profusion of flowers—anemones, carnations, chrysanthemums, dahlias, daisies, foxgloves, iris, lilies, peonies, roses, and tulips—with fruits and vegetables. Alabaster urns, pewter jars, bronze ewers or urns, green or amber glass, silver bowls, and baskets were all used as containers, often nearly hidden by the flowers, foliage, and fruits spilling over the edge. Accessories of bird's nests and eggs, butterflies, stuffed squirrels, books, or common household items were often placed on the table, further obscuring the container. Popular colors were vibrant and usually warm yellows, oranges, and reds with cobalt blue, purple, and soft greens as complements.

French

Designs of the French period (17th and 18th centuries) were the least weighty of the Mass designs of Europe. They had as common characteristics formal balance, greater height than width, harmony rather than contrast, and soft colors. Porcelain fruit baskets, vases, compotes or urns of crystal, Venetian glass, bronze, alabaster, or silver were used with many kinds of garden flowers. Spike flowers, such as delphiniums, larkspur, lilacs, or stock, were often combined with trailing tendrils. Roses and other sweetly scented flowers were favored. Arrangements had no center of interest and no grouping of kinds and colors.

Georgian

The Georgian period (18th and early 19th centuries) is further divided stylistically into designs of the Early Georgian (1714–1760) and Late Georgian (1760–1820) periods. Early Georgian containers were generally heavy metal or marble urns. Plant material in rich, warm colors—tulips, lilacs, fruit blossoms, columbine, and grasses—were often used. Late Georgian designs differed in that the colors became more delicate and designs showed a strong French influence. Designs were triangular in form with perfect symmetry.

Victorian

Victorian (19th century) designs, the most compact of all Mass arrangements, were globular or circular in form. Bold, rich colors or all-white arrangements were common. Unlike those in the French style, designs were often wider than they were tall. Circular nosegays became popular at this time, and special folding stands were made expressly for them so that they did not have to be held continuously. Fruits and foliage, without flowers, were sometimes arranged in various kinds of Victorian glass, rose bowls, silver, Haviland china, or Belleek porcelain. Figurines, Currier and Ives prints, photo albums, prayer books, sewing boxes, or music boxes were often used as accessories.

A Traditional Mass design in the French style.

A Traditional Mass design inspired by the Early Georgian period and held aloft in a heavy metal container. This arrangement shows effective use of polychromatic color harmony. Design by Deen Day Smith, Atlanta, Georgia.

AMERICAN DESIGNS

European designs are an important part of our heritage: the floral designs of the time and times past were brought to America with the early settlers, and those that followed continued to exert a transatlantic influence. Times were difficult in the colonies, with fewer and different plant materials available, a revolution brewing, and a breaking-away from most things European. For a time, there was little more than the gathering of a few garden flowers and herbs into simple bouquet forms. Soon, however, distinctly American styles emerged, developing in tandem with the changing tastes of Europe.

Colonial

The designs of the Colonial period (17th century) were typically informal mixed bouquets arranged in household utensils of pewter, copper, brass, or earthenware, or in baskets or wooden bowls. Dried materials were often combined with scented herb foliage and common garden flowers.

Colonial Williamsburg

The designs of 18th-century Colonial Williamsburg (1720–1780) were generally fan-shaped, with flowers lightly arranged at the top and closely spaced at the rim of the container. The overall effect was one of elegance. Fresh flowers were often combined with wheat or barley, and plant material sometimes completely concealed the container. Containers were English in style, of bronze, alabaster, marble, pewter, silver, or porcelain. Fruits and flowers were sometimes placed on the table beside the design.

Federal

The Federal style (late 18th and early 19th centuries) is typified by Mass designs with formal balance having greater height than width and showing more French influence than English. Fruits were combined with flowers and foliage. Containers were often vases, epergnes, urns, or compotes of pressed glass, silver, or porcelain. Figurines, candlesticks, paintings, or other household items were often displayed alongside the flower arrangement.

American Victorian

Early in the American Victorian period (late 19th century), styles followed the general characteristics of European Victorian designs. The lavish use of flowers in ornate containers was followed by a period of oversimplification. Rather than a planned design, a dozen carnations were often placed in a glass vase with some ornamental asparagus fern.

Early 20th-Century American

The early 1930s saw the first great interest in floral design as a creative outlet. The garden club movement began in earnest, and both garden and florist's flowers were readily available. It was from the strong influences of the Oriental Line and European Mass, translated directly into Line and Mass designs respectively, that a new style of floral design was developed in the United States. This new style is commonly referred to as a Line-mass design.

The Early 20th-Century American designs of Line, Line-mass, and Mass are still popular today and will be covered in more detail in later chapters. All were created using set patterns, strict rules, and previously executed styles. They are

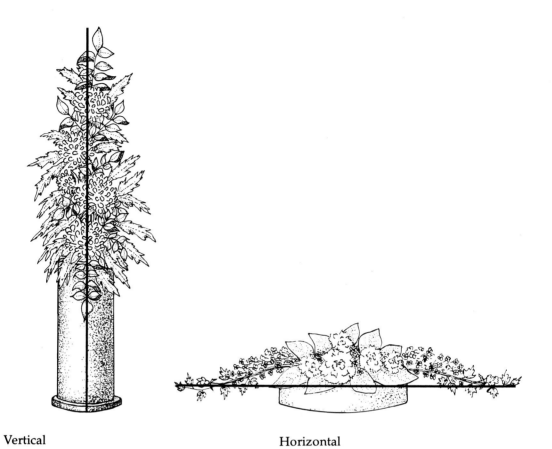

Vertical   Horizontal

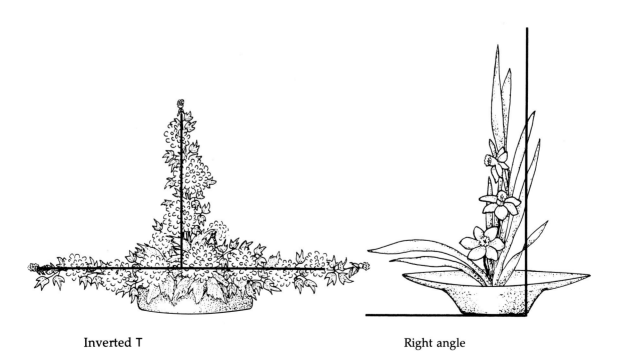

Inverted T   Right angle

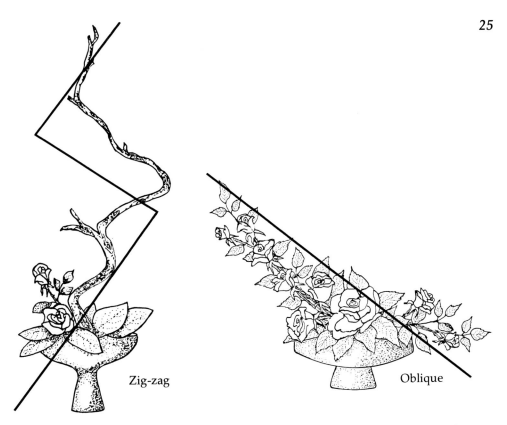

Zig-zag   Oblique

based on geometric forms and have one focal area at or near the point of emergence. To include an even number of any one plant material is considered improper.

Line designs are adapted from the Oriental Line designs in which the linear pattern is dominant. The silhouette is open form, requiring great restraint in the amount of plant material used. Line designs may be vertical, horizontal, crescent, Hogarth (S-curve), zig-zag, oblique, or the popular asymmetrical triangle with its right- or left-handed variants. Vertical and horizontal line directions in combination yield the inverted T and the right angle. These designs all follow set patterns and allow little room for creativity other than in the combination of plant material, texture, and color. There is a single focal area and one point of emergence. Most often the length of the longest line material is one-and-one-half times the height or diameter of the container, whichever is greater.

Line-mass (or massed-line) designs, merging the best qualities of Oriental Line and Occidental Mass, have an open silhouette. Additional plant material is used, or massed, to enhance and strengthen the line. The dominant line, for instance, is fortified with a mass of plant material at the focal area. Line-mass designs follow the vertical, horizontal, or other line directions of Line designs. A set pattern is followed. Creativity is expressed in the choice of plant material, color, and texture, or an unusual combination of materials. Again, the longest line is usually one-and-one-half times the height or diameter of the container.

Mass designs were adapted from the European Mass designs and use a large quantity of plant material. This type of design has a closed silhouette and almost always has symmetrical balance. Mass designs are oval, circular, fan-shaped, or triangular in form. Plant material is placed in a less compact manner than in European Mass designs. There is always only one focal area. Distinction is accomplished by the selection of plant materials for the design; designs may be of only one or two kinds of flowers, or entirely of foliage.

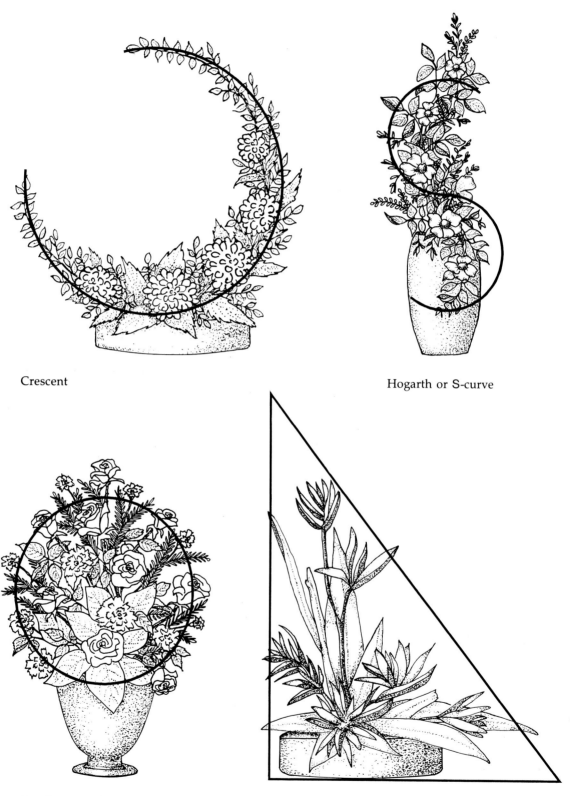

Crescent

Hogarth or S-curve

Circular or oval

Asymmetrical triangle

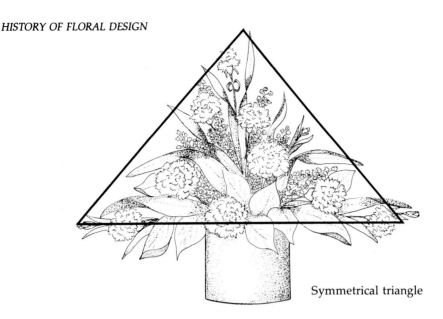

Symmetrical triangle

Our brief history is fast approaching the present and future of floral design. In the 1950s some arrangers felt increasingly restricted by the rules and set patterns of the Early 20th-Century American designs, now nearly synonymous with the Traditional designs upon which they were based. While one group of arrangers was content to stay with the period designs, others broke away in another direction. They began to look at other contemporary art forms, seeking new ideas and inspiration. As they explored other arts, arrangers began to see their own medium in a new light. No longer were certain combinations, set patterns, and naturalistic placement a mandate. Floral designers realized that flower arranging is a creative outlet and a true, evolving art form; they modernized it accordingly.

Plant material was used to express a feeling; set a mood; make a statement; create an idea; or capture the essence or inner meaning of a subject. Arrangers became fascinated with abstract art and began to apply the painterly concept of abstraction to floral design. Plant material was abstracted into an often unnatural placement or form by clipping, tying, looping, folding, stripping, bending, or knotting. Interest was distributed throughout the design rather than in a single focal area.

Non-Traditional designs were categorized as modern, contemporary, avant-garde, or creative. *Creative design* is the term that has been most consistently used. National Council of State Garden Clubs—an international organization founded in 1929 and based in the United States—currently lists all designs as either Traditional or Creative (which includes abstract). It has assumed the leadership role in floral design in the United States as have its International Affiliate clubs in other countries.

Creative designs place less restrictions on the arranger—who need only follow the principles of design and the flower show schedule, if the design is for exhibition—and are becoming more and more popular.

No one country has a monopoly on Creative designs. Each has much to offer, and styles are eagerly adopted by designers in other countries, often through floral design schools and organizations. With the present-day ease of travel and rapid communication between countries, designers around the world share, with equal parts of speed and goodwill, their love of flowers and latest expressions in floral design.

2 The Basics: Containers, Mechanics, and Plant Material

Flowers, with their varied colors, forms, and fragrance, are an attractive addition to our indoor surroundings, raising our spirits through this unexpected association with nature. Fresh flowers have an intangible quality that most people find appealing; it may be that we identify with their transitory nature. For whatever reason, flowers add an expression of love and caring to any setting.

Anyone can arrange flowers; however, success will depend upon three basic items: containers, mechanics (methods of control), and plant material.

CONTAINERS

Containers should suit the specific design desired, both in color and texture, and befit the final setting of the arrangement. For instance, the arranger with a rather formal lifestyle or whose home is furnished with antiques would be wise to select containers compatible with his or her own particular situation. Traditional compotes, urns, or cylinders of ceramic, silver, or glass will be most appropriate. Flower arrangements should tend toward the Traditional, with symmetrical Mass designs being the most suitable style.

A wider variety of container types are appropriate for those with contemporary or eclectic home furnishings and a less-formal entertaining style. The eclectic home already combines many styles, giving the arranger a wide range of choice in both containers and designs. Containers may be of ceramic, glass, or metal. Simple compotes; low, round bowls; oblong or square containers; or columns of one solid color are all possibilities. Modern or non-Traditional containers with rough or smooth textures and several openings will be effective.

The futuristic home requires non-Traditional containers suitable for Creative or Abstract designs. Containers should be very sleek and modern, with many openings, and may be of metal, glass, or ceramic. There may be more than one point of emergence; it is not necessary, however, to have plant material emerge from all container openings.

Though they may still be difficult to find in some areas, there appears to be a renewal of interest in ceramic and glass containers; many are currently available

A collection of Traditional and contemporary containers.

in department stores and florist shops. Because they are mass-produced, all of a type are quite uniform in quality, form, and color. These are suitable for the beginning arranger and are sometimes used in multiples for very creative work. Avoid plastic containers or any with decorations, bright colors, a shiny surface (especially copper or brass), or a narrow opening. Likewise avoid those shaped like animals, or everyday objects such as shoes or toys.

As the flower arranger becomes more skilled and interested in Creative designs, the common container no longer appeals. A visit to an arts-and-crafts show or a local potter may provide some one-of-a-kind containers. Some arrangers develop a second avenue of creative expression by making their own unique containers.

The beginner should invest in a few unadorned containers of basic shapes and styles; it is wise to spend as little as possible at first rather than buy many containers only to find later that most are not suitable. In Traditional flower arranging, the container should blend with the plant material and not compete with the design; a decorated container is not recommended as it tends to draw attention away from the plant material. In Creative designs, the container takes on more importance and may actually be featured.

As to color, though one may assume that "white goes with everything," there can be a problem with visual weight and stability. White is also visually attracting, and a white container may overpower the design. Including a few white flowers in a design arranged in a white container will unify the plant material and container. Containers with a dull, matte finish—in earth tones such as brown, black,

A collection of the more unusual containers used in Creative work. Each has several openings, although not all are visible in the photograph.

gray, or dark green—are most useful for the beginner. More colorful containers, in more varied styles, may be added to the collection as experience and an individual style are developed.

Choose containers that hold water; those that do not, labeled "for dried material only" or "will not hold water," may be used as long as those warnings are observed. Look also for containers with openings large enough to allow for the easy insertion of plant material. All too often the appealingly tall, slender container has such a small opening that it is impossible to use.

A shallow, oblong or round container; a compote; a tall, slender cylinder— all are basic styles and easy to use for the first-time arranger. Baskets are attractive and useful for dried plant material; even fresh plant material may be used in a basket by placing a bowl inside to hold the needleholder or oasis. This will protect the basket from moisture.

Containers may be something never intended for that purpose, such as empty wine bottles, flat baking dishes, shallow silver bowls, candlesticks, or candelabra. As one develops expertise in flower arranging, contriving containers from such items becomes both interesting and rewarding.

Even more unlikely components can be fashioned into a perfectly useful container. Downspout can be cut into a desired length and set vertically, with a piece of lumber pushed up into the bottom for weight and another of plywood, a few inches larger than the downspout, firmly attached as a base for stability. Insert a small can in the top for the needleholder. Spray it flat black, and it is hard to believe the resulting container is made entirely from discarded items.

Pieces of solid styrofoam packing can be attached to one another to make an abstract container. A brick in the bottom adds weight and stability. Cover the form with artist's gesso to protect it; some paints cause styrofoam to disintegrate. Allow the gesso to dry before painting the desired color. Very little expense is involved, and the result is a one-of-a-kind container which will be fun to use and add a further touch of creativity to a design.

Many designs are enhanced by a footed container. With a minimum of effort as well as expense, such a container can be made by turning a lovely goblet upside down and arranging a bowl or deep plate on top. Floral clay will temporarily adhere the two; epoxy glue may be used to permanently bond the elegant result.

Lamp bases; car springs and other machinery parts; plastic or PVC piping; old bird cages; tree branches; pieces of weathered wood; large sea shells—these and many other found pieces are a different sort of challenge to our creativity. All can be given a new life with a little imagination and perhaps a coat of paint.

Bamboo mats, decorative · wood, forms of plexiglass or wood, Oriental stands, scroll stands, or woven mats are often used as a base under a container and the design it holds. Whatever the composition of each, the base and the container become one and are considered a single component. A base should be used only when it serves a specific purpose, however. It may provide visual stability or function as a connective to unify multiple containers, or a container and accessories. It may aid the rhythmic flow of a design or assist in achieving a proper proportion. A well-chosen base may help establish dominance, or contrast of color, form, or texture. It may reinforce the degree of formality or otherwise establish the character of a design. Perhaps a design's theme will be better interpreted with the aid of a particular base. Finally, a base may reduce the bottom-heaviness of a design by incorporating space beneath it. Bases are used more often with Traditional designs than with Creative designs.

MECHANICS

Most containers will require some means, beyond the simple aperture, of holding plant material in the desired position. Mechanics are best described as devices used to control plant material in a container and must be neat, clean, and unobtrusive. From a needleholder to floral foam to chicken wire, each has its own uses, singly and in combination with other devices. Experience and experimentation will allow the designer to begin collecting these various and essential items. It is helpful to have a basket, box, or something similar in which to organize mechanics and keep them handy. A fishing tackle box works well, with a place for everything, and the box is easily stored or carried to a flower show, if desired. Nothing is more exasperating than time spent searching for a misplaced item.

Needleholders (also known as pinholders or kenzans) are the most popular means of controlling plant material. They come in various shapes, such as round, oval, oblong, or square. The inexpensive ones on the market are almost completely useless and totally frustrating. A good needleholder has a heavy lead base, is straight-sided (the base does not extend beyond the needles), and has many sharp, pointed, closely spaced needles or pins. The "cheapies" are often bright green in color and have dull needles spaced far apart; they are a waste of time and money. It is better to spend a little more at the outset and have mechanics that will work well and last for many years.

Some needleholders are made especially for decorative wood. A screw attaches the wood to a needleholder with the needles pointing down; this needleholder is lowered onto another needleholder which has been placed in a container in the usual manner with the points up. These holders work best for relatively small, well-balanced pieces of wood. Large, very heavy, or unbalanced pieces will require special mechanics. These will be discussed in the next chapter.

A pin straightener is useful should needles become bent, a common result when a heavy branch is impaled over them. This tool is small enough to fit over individual pins and easily mislaid. Keeping it on a key ring will prevent it from becoming lost.

When selecting a needleholder for a particular design, choose the smallest one possible as it will not require so much effort to keep it hidden. Plant material or other components should always be used according to the principles of design, not merely as a cover-up for oversized mechanics. Adding material for the sole purpose of covering the mechanics can destroy an otherwise pleasing arrangement. It is far better to have neat mechanics slightly visible than to add components not essential to the design.

Needleholders are available in brown, black, and a very dark, dull green. If the needleholder is used in a container of another color, it is sometimes helpful to spray it the same color as the container, or as close to that color as possible, making it less noticeable.

Cupholders are another essential mechanic. The needleholder in this case is permanently attached inside a cup which will hold sufficient water for fresh plant material. They are made of lead and are available in the same shapes and colors as regular needleholders. The sides should be straight rather than flare out. Cupholders are used on flat surfaces where water would otherwise be unavailable for plant material; they are not necessary in containers that will hold water. If cupholders are not available, or in an emergency, substitute a small flat can, such as a tuna fish can, paint it an appropriate color, and fit it with a needleholder attached to the inside. Flower arrangers will need both regular needleholders and cupholders.

Lead cupholders are heavy enough to remain in position, but needleholders will require floral clay to anchor them in the container. Both the needleholder and the container must be perfectly dry for the clay to adhere. Floral clay is available in white or green; either color will do as the clay must be used in a manner that keeps it out of view. Roll a small piece of this sticky clay between your palms until it is long and slender and fashion it into a circle slightly smaller than the needleholder. Press the clay firmly to the bottom of the needleholder, about a quarter of an inch from the edge, making sure the ends meet. Using a small hand towel or oven mitt to protect your hand from the sharp needles, place the needleholder in the container and press down firmly, giving it a slight twist to force attachment to the container. It is timesaving to own enough needleholders to leave them attached to the containers used most often. If the needleholder must be removed, scrape away as much of the floral clay as possible. Lighter fluid or a spray-type laundry stain remover will eliminate any that remains.

A tall, cylindrical container can be a problem when a needleholder is required. If the needleholder is placed in the bottom of the container, plant material with very long stems is necessary and placement of material is difficult. Better to fill the container with kitty litter to within three or four inches of the top. Pour a layer of paraffin over the kitty litter to form a solid base and place a cupholder atop it. Some arrangers find that a piece of crushed, one-inch chicken wire inserted into a tall container works just as well. Others find this method does not offer adequate control of the plant material.

Floral foams are sometimes useful for difficult containers. Oasis is used for fresh plant material; sahara is made especially for dried plant material and cannot be used for fresh plant material as it does not absorb water. They do have their disadvantages, however. Once a hole has been made in foam it is there to stay, and the foam soon becomes fragile and useless. Certain plant material will not last well in foam as the stem ends become clogged with it and can no longer take up water; roses are a prime example.

Oasis must be placed in water until it is thoroughly saturated, then cut to fit snugly inside the container. If the oasis fits tightly and does not extend above the top of the container, no attachment is required. If, however, the foam extends above the top of the container, it can be kept in place using the floral tape made especially for use with oasis. Place two strips of tape at right angles to each other across the oasis and down over the rim of the container for about an inch. This will hold the foam firmly in place. Some designers use one-inch chicken wire or thin plastic wrap around the oasis to help it hold its form. This is particularly important when the foam does not fit inside the container.

When arranging flowers in a Mass design it sometimes helps to use oasis and a needleholder together. Attach the needleholder to the container in the usual manner, then place a square of old nylon pantyhose over the needles, extending it out slightly over the edge of the needleholder. The oasis is then placed on the needleholder. Heavy pieces of plant material can be impaled through the foam onto the needles; smaller plant material may go only into the foam. With this pairing, more plant material can be accommodated and may be placed at angles that would be very difficult if a needleholder were the only mechanic. When the arrangement has served its purpose and the container is being cleaned for storage, grasp the nylon and pull it off the needles; the oasis will come neatly off as well. Those who have had the unfortunate experience of trying to remove oasis from a needleholder without nylon between the two will not look forward to a repeat performance.

Sometimes oasis is used on a candelabrum in order to provide moisture to plant material where a cupholder would be out of the question. Wrap the soaked oasis in thin plastic wrap and cover the entire piece with one-inch chicken wire. Tape or wire the foam to the candelabrum, taking care all will be hidden from view when the design is completed. Wrapping the oasis in this manner will prevent it from falling apart. It may be necessary to prick a hole in the plastic wrap in order to insert the plant material.

Transparent glass containers are difficult from the standpoint of concealing mechanics. Sometimes a needleholder is hidden by placing cracked marbles around its base. Never use floral foam in a glass container as the foam is unsightly.

Other essentials for a basic flower-arranging kit are florist's wire of various sizes; flower arranger's clippers; a sharp knife; floral tape; transparent tape; a glue gun (useful for attaching decorative wood and dried plant material); and extra glue sticks. When an item proves useful, put it in the kit so it is readily available. Experienced arrangers will have gathered many more items in their flower-arranging kits, such as an extension cord; pliers; a hammer; wooden chopsticks to extend stem length; squares of old nylons; water picks; and orchid tubes. Good mechanics are the basis for every good design. Without a workable method of controlling plant material, the arranger is doomed from the start.

PLANT MATERIAL

Fresh plant material is most often employed; however, a supply of dried and/or treated plant material is useful in the winter months, especially for those residing in cold climates. The garden may be a constant source of plant material, either used while fresh or dried for later use. How much plant material one can grow depends upon the size of the garden. Even the apartment or condominium dweller may be able to grow some plants in containers on a balcony, deck, or patio.

Florist's flowers are another possibility, but there are some disadvantages—among them the expense and the lack of gradation in stages of development. Whereas nature offers the full range, rarely can a florist provide at once the buds, partially open, and fully open blooms of a given flower. Flowers purchased from the florist should have a half inch of stem removed before being placed in tepid water (approximately 110° F). A fresh cut allows the stems to take on more water which in turn makes them last longer in the design. Some arrangers use a commercial preservative in the water, available from the florist. Others use a home-made preservative of one gallon of warm water, one tablespoon bottled lemon juice, one tablespoon sugar, and one teaspoon chlorine bleach. Preservatives benefit both florist's flowers and those cut from the home garden.

The supermarket is another potential source of plant material. Many grocery stores now handle flowers, and their fruits and vegetables can be attractively combined with foliage and/or fresh flowers.

Fresh line and filler material—branches and foliage such as iris, phormium, and ivy—needn't come from the florist. One's own garden or those of friends or neighbors are likely sources of this essential plant material.

Line is the basic foundation of design, and the floral designer usually begins by establishing the structural framework of the planned design. Linear plant material is most often used, although decorative wood may be substituted. In Creative designs man-made items, such as wire, plastic, rope, or metal, may provide the line material. Each type of line material has its uses in floral design. In designs for the home, the materials used are the designer's choice. In a flower show, the schedule may determine what is allowable.

Careful selection of linear plant material will make it easier to produce the desired direction in a design. Branches that grow vertically naturally are best used in a vertical manner in the design; branches growing diagonally in nature do best in diagonal placement; for a line curving to the left, look for one on the plant that grows naturally in that direction. It is quicker, easier, and less frustrating to search for the proper direction of growth than to manipulate the plant material.

Some flowers have linear form, such as delphinium, foxglove, gladiolus, larkspur, lupine, physostegia, salvia, stock, tritoma, or others with similar characteristics. Each of these is limited to some degree by its blooming season.

There are many more non-floral candidates for linear material such as grasses or vines, or the foliage or branches of many trees, flowers, herbs, and shrubs. Azalea, cattails, climbing hydrangea, copper or tricolor beech, crab apple, iris (such as spuria), magnolia, phormium, pine, pussy willow, spiral eucalyptus, umbrella pine, and many more evergreen and deciduous materials are possible substitutes for flowers. Deciduous branches are often just as lovely bare as they are with foliage and/or blooms.

Transitional, or filler, plant material generally has smaller blooms and is

rounded or spray-type in form, such as baby's breath, certain small chrysanthemums, ferns, and heathers. In Creative designs, the use of transitional
materials is rare.

Round forms occur much more often in flowers than linear forms or transitional materials. These featured forms are either round or cone-shaped in outline, such as chrysanthemums, daffodils, dahlias, lilies, rhododendrons, and roses.

Each of these forms has a role to play in floral design, and it is hoped that
every floral designer will choose to fill these various roles with real plant material
rather than artificial flowers and foliage. All garden club members are encouraged
to use the real thing in arrangements, even if it must be dried rather than fresh.
There may be a place for silk flowers, but they are not permitted in flower shows.

Cutting plant material

Plant material should be cut in late afternoon or early evening as this is the
time when plant sugars and moisture are at their highest levels. Early morning is
an alternate time but not quite as good as late afternoon. For fresh plant material,
midday is least desirable as plant sugars and moisture are at their lowest; if the
plant material will be dried for later use, however, this is the ideal time to cut.
Even plant material cut at the optimum time should be conditioned overnight
before use.

Almost all plant material may be safely cut with very sharp clippers or a
sharp knife. With dahlias, however, a sharp knife is best, and chrysanthemum
stems should always be broken, not cut. Heavy pruning shears may be needed for
large branches. Sharpness is the key with any cutting tool as it prevents the
bruising and tearing of plant tissues which may lead to early decay. Carry a deep
container of water into the garden and place cut material into the water immediately. Stems should then be recut under water at an angle. The angle cut
prevents the stem from fitting tightly against the bottom of the container and
sealing off the supply of water; recutting under water prevents an air bubble from
forming at the cut end which would prevent water being taken up into the stem.

Flowers that unfold, such as iris, daylilies, and poppies, have a limited life
span and should be cut when color is showing in the bud and petals have begun
to loosen. Blooms that open and enlarge slowly, like roses, are cut when they are
beginning to open but before the center is expanded. Foliage that will be submerged in the finished design should be removed. Soft, fuzzy foliage must always
be removed as it becomes waterlogged and quickly deteriorates under water.

Experience will be the best teacher in learning to gauge the proper stage of
development for cutting a specific plant material. Recommendations for some of
the types most useful to flower arrangers will be found in the list of conditioning
methods beginning on the next page.

Conditioning plant material

When the plant material has been taken indoors and the stems recut under
water, almost all varieties should be put in deep, tepid water, with or without a
preservative, and placed in a cool spot, out of drafts. It is best to allow plant
material to condition overnight before use in a design. A minimum of several
hours is always necessary.

Some plant material requires special treatment in order to condition well,
more than those basic requirements just described. Hollow-stemmed flowers, like
delphiniums and amaryllis, should be turned upside down and the stems filled
with water. Plug the stem end with cotton, or simply hold a finger over the end

and invert the stem, placing it in the pail of water and removing the finger after the stem end is submerged.

Stems which exude a milky substance, like poppies, poinsettias, and other euphorbias, will require searing to seal the ends. To do this, hold the stem end over a candle flame until it is blackened or put the end of the stem in boiling water for about twenty seconds. Protect the foliage and bloom by wrapping them in tissue paper. This searing procedure must be repeated every time the stem is recut. Pinholders are not suitable for use with this type of plant material as the needles pierce the stem, destroying the seal.

Dahlias are conditioned by placing about two inches of the stem end in very hot water (approximately 180° F). Allow the water to cool, then plunge the stems up to the neck in tepid water overnight.

Daffodils and hyacinths exude a substance that is destructive to other flowers. They should therefore be conditioned in separate containers for several hours before placement with other blooms.

Woody stems should have approximately one inch of bark removed at the bottom and then be split at right angles or crushed to expose more stem to take up water. Place in deep, tepid water overnight.

In early spring, some kinds of shrub and tree branches can be forced into bloom by cutting and bringing them indoors. Choose branches that show enlarged bloom buds, remove the bark from the bottom inch of the stem, then split the stem at right angles. Place stems in several inches of warm water and mist the branches every day. The length of time required for blooms to open will depend upon the stage of development at the time of cutting. This cannot be predicted accurately and is a matter of experimentation.

Containers and other vessels used for conditioning plant materials or holding designs should be kept scrupulously clean. After each use, wash them thoroughly with warm, soapy water to which a little chlorine bleach has been added. Rinse well and dry before storage.

The list that follows is a guide to conditioning methods for flowers and foliage commonly used in flower arranging, although they are not the only successful means. When relevant, a recommendation for the optimum time for cutting plant material is given as well. Unless otherwise specified, all plant material is conditioned in deep water.

Acer palmatum (JAPANESE MAPLE)
Cut only mature foliage; strip bottom inch of bark; split stem ends; tepid water.

Achillea (YARROW)
Cut before all florets are open; remove foliage; tepid water.

Agapanthus (includes LILY-OF-THE-NILE)
Cut when one-fourth of florets are open; tepid water.

Akebia
Crush stem ends; tepid water.

Allium (includes CHIVES; ORNAMENTAL GARLIC)
Cut when only a few florets are open; change water often.

Alstroemeria (PERUVIAN LILY)
Remove foliage; tepid water with preservative.

Anemone (WINDFLOWER)
Cut while centers are tight; tepid water.

Anthurium (FLAMINGO FLOWER)
>Tepid water.

Antirrhinum (SNAPDRAGON)
>Cut when one-half of florets are open; place in the dark or directly under a bright light to keep tips straight, or wrap in florist waxed paper; tepid water.

Aquilegia (COLUMBINE)
>Cut before blooms are fully open; tepid water.

Aster (MICHAELMAS DAISY)
>Sear stem ends; remove foliage; tepid water.

Astilbe (SPIREA)
>Cut when one-half of florets are open; split stem ends; tepid water.

Azalea
>Strip bottom inch of bark; split or crush stem ends; tepid water.

Calendula (includes POT MARIGOLD)
>Cut when two-thirds to three-fourths of blooms are open; remove foliage under water line; tepid water.

Calluna (SCOTCH HEATHER)
>Cut when blooms first open; split stem ends; tepid water.

Camellia
>Cut when blooms are just beginning to open; split stem ends; handle carefully as blooms shatter readily; tepid water.

Chaenomeles (includes JAPANESE QUINCE)
>Strip bottom inch of bark; split stem ends; tepid water.

Chrysanthemum
>Break stem ends; split large stem ends; tepid water.

Clematis
>Sear stem ends; tepid water.

Cordyline terminalis (TI)
>Tepid water.

Dahlia
>Remove foliage under water line; place bottom two or three inches of stem in very hot water; allow water to cool; plunge neck-deep in tepid water and leave overnight.

Delphinium (LARKSPUR)
>Fill hollow stems with tepid water; plug stem ends with cotton; tepid water.

Dianthus (PINK; includes CARNATION)
>Break stems at joint; tepid water.

Enkianthus
>Strip bottom inch of bark; split stem ends; tepid water.

Eremurus (FOXTAIL LILY)
>Cut when one-half of florets are open; tepid water.

Eucalyptus
>Split stem ends; tepid water.

Euphorbia (includes POINSETTIA)
>Sear stem ends; tepid water.

Evergreen foliage
>Strip bottom inch of bark; split stem ends; tepid water.

Fatsia
>Tepid water.

Fern
> Submerge in tepid water.

Forsythia
> Strip bottom inch of bark; split stem ends; tepid water.

Fuchsia
> Split stem ends; tepid water.

Gaillardia (BLANKET FLOWER)
> Cut while centers are tight; split stem ends; remove foliage under water line; tepid water.

Gerbera (includes TRANSVAAL DAISY)
> Split stem ends; wrap stems in florist waxed paper to keep stems straight; tepid water with preservative containing sugar.

Gladiolus
> Cut when three or four florets are open; split stem ends; place in the dark or wrap in florist waxed paper to keep tips straight; small tip-end buds are sometimes removed because they may turn toward light in the finished design; tepid water.

Gloriosa (GLORY LILY)
> Split stem ends; tepid water.

Gypsophila (includes BABY'S BREATH)
> Cut when three-fourths of florets are open; tepid water.

Hamamelis (WITCH HAZEL)
> Strip bottom inch of bark; split stem ends; tepid water.

Hedera (IVY)
> Submerge in tepid water.

Heliconia (LOBSTER-CLAW)
> Split stem ends; tepid water.

Helleborus (HELLEBORE; includes CHRISTMAS ROSE)
> Difficult to condition; sear stem ends or submerge; tepid water.

Hemerocallis (DAYLILY)
> Tepid water.

Hippeastrum (AMARYLLIS)
> Fill hollow stems with water; plug stem ends with cotton; tepid water.

Hosta (PLANTAIN LILY; FUNKIA)
> Split stem ends of bloom stalk; submerge foliage in tepid water.

Hyacinthus (HYACINTH)
> Cut when one-half of florets are open; place in separate container as hyacinths exude a substance that is harmful to other plant material; tepid water.

Hydrangea
> Split stem ends; tepid water.

Ilex (HOLLY)
> Strip bottom inch of bark; split stem ends; tepid water.

Iris (includes BEARDED, DUTCH, SPANISH)
> Tepid water with preservative containing sugar.

Kniphofia (RED-HOT-POKER)
> Cut when one-half of florets are open; tepid water.

Lavandula (LAVENDER)
> Cut when one-half of florets are open; shallow, tepid water.

Liatris (GAY-FEATHER)
Split stem ends; tepid water.

Lilium (LILY)
Split stem ends; remove foliage under water line; remove anthers if desired; tepid water.

Lupinus (LUPINE)
Cut when one-half of florets are open; remove foliage under water line; fill hollow stems with water; plug stem ends with cotton; tepid water.

Magnolia
Cut before blooms open; strip bottom inch of bark; split stem ends; tepid water.

Malus (APPLE, includes CRAB APPLE)
Cut when one-fourth of florets are open; strip bottom inch of bark; split or crush stem ends; tepid water.

Nandina
Strip bottom inch of bark; split stem ends; tepid water.

Narcissus (DAFFODIL)
Cut before blooms open; place in separate container as daffodils exude a substance that is harmful to other plant material; wrap stem ends with transparent tape to prevent splitting and curling; tepid water.

Orchid
Cut when blooms are fully open; avoid wetting blooms; tepid water.

Paeonia (PEONY)
Cut before blooms are fully open; split stem ends; tepid water with preservative containing sugar.

Papaver (POPPY)
Cut when blooms are just beginning to open; sear stem ends; tepid water with preservative containing sugar.

Pelargonium (GERANIUM)
Remove foliage under water line; tepid water.

Phormium tenax (NEW ZEALAND FLAX)
Tepid water.

Protea
Split stem ends; dip stem ends in boiling water; tepid water.

Prunus (includes FLOWERING PLUM, CHERRY, PEACH)
Cut branches with single blooms when one-fourth of blooms are open; cut branches with double blooms when one-half of blooms are open; strip bottom inch of bark; split stem ends; tepid water.

Rhododendron
Cut while center of truss is still in tight bud; split or crush stem ends; tepid water.

Rosa (ROSE)
Cut when blooms are one-third to one-half open; split stem ends; tepid water.

Salix (includes PUSSY WILLOW)
Strip bottom inch of bark; split stem ends; tepid water only if further development is desired.

Scilla (BLUE BELL; SQUILL)
Cut when one-half to two-thirds of florets are open; tepid water with preservative containing sugar.

Strelitzia (BIRD-OF-PARADISE)
> Tepid water with preservative.

Syringa (LILAC)
> Cut when one-third to one-half of florets are open; remove foliage; split stem ends; tepid water with preservative.

Tagetes (MARIGOLD)
> Cut while centers are tight; remove foliage; tepid water.

Tulipa (TULIP)
> Cut while still in bud but beginning to loosen; wrap tightly in cone of butcher paper or cellophane to keep stems straight; tepid water containing one tablespoon gin per quart of water.

Zantedeschia (CALLA)
> Submerge leaves; condition bloom in tepid water.

Zinnia
> Cut while centers are tight; remove foliage under water line; sear stem ends; tepid water.

Grooming plant material

Cleanliness and the damage done by pests and diseases are both important concerns in flower arranging. We may trust the florist for quality, but if plant material is grown in the home garden, measures must be taken to attain the one and prevent the other. Detailed advice on how to avoid insects, infections, and even physiological disorders is best gotten from professionals, such as local extension agents, and the many books which treat the topic. But once successfully raised, grooming plant material for cleanliness is a relatively simple matter. At the conditioning stage, check the material for soil and spray residue. Evergreen foliage is easily washed in some warm water to which a small amount of liquid detergent has been added. Swish the foliage in the water, rinse with plain water, and allow to dry. It is important that the water in which the foliage is rinsed is at least as warm as that in which it was washed, or there will be a detergent residue left on the surface of leaves or needles. Remember that evergreen foliage has had several seasons outdoors in all kinds of weather; even if it looks clean, this may not always be the case. Washing the material will give it a clean, fresh look that will enhance the beauty of the design. Any foliage with a firm surface texture may be washed if necessary; however, unless it is very soiled, wiping with a soft cloth or brush will clean it adequately. Soft, fuzzy foliage must not be washed as the process may cause water spots, remove some of the delicate cilia, or cause discoloration.

Drying plant material

Dried plant material is plant material from which all moisture has been removed. There are several ways drying may be accomplished: by natural means, either hanging or upright; by the use of a drying agent, or dessicant; or in the microwave oven with a dessicant. With few exceptions, more color is retained with the use of a drying agent, with or without a microwave oven.

Garden flowers and foliage, florist's flowers, wild grasses, seed pods, ferns, and herbs are all treasures for the flower arranger. Cones and seed pods dry naturally, but many flowers and certain foliage will require special treatment.

When gathering plant material in the wild, be sure to respect private property and state conservation lists.

Dried plant material is extremely versatile and may serve the arranger in a variety of ways. Although we are primarily concerned with its use in flower arranging, such plant material is also employed in wreaths, pressed flower pictures, potpourri, wall hangings, and so on. The time to gather plant material for any of these purposes is the same; only the treatment following the harvest will vary.

Plant material meant for drying should be cut on a bright, sunny day after the dew has had a chance to evaporate—usually about midday, when the moisture content within the plant tissues is low. Cut material at the peak of its development; if plant material is past its prime, petals may drop or shatter and your time has been wasted. A few buds at various stages of development are helpful when arranging, but blooms that are partially or fully open are more often required.

Stem length is optional and based primarily on the plant material involved and its intended use. Some flowers and foliage are best cut with their stems long enough to be retained; others will need to have stems replaced with wire. Wire stems covered with floral tape are very pliable; this is an advantage over natural stems, which cannot be adjusted for better placement. Regardless of the drying method used, remove all excess foliage as it slows the drying process.

Some blooms will dry well when tied into small bunches and hung upside down in a warm, dark place. When air-drying flowers, a general rule is the smaller the individual stems, the more may be tied in a single bunch. Avoid tying so many stems together that flowers are crowded, destroying their natural form. Once the plant material is dry, the form is permanent and cannot be changed.

Remove all foliage and side stems that will not be useful. Tie stems together securely; rubber bands are an excellent choice for this, keeping the stems held tightly together as they tend to shrivel during the drying process. Attach a piece of string to the rubber band to allow for hanging. Keep bunches separated; good circulation of air hastens drying. The quicker the flowers dry, the more color will be retained, so the ideal drying location is in a warm, dark place where there is good air circulation. An attic or a large closet would both suit. Some flowers dry better when left standing upright in a container with about an inch of water which is allowed to evaporate as the flowers dry. Bells-of-Ireland, hydrangeas, and heathers all dry best using this method. Hydrangeas need to dry very quickly in order to retain their color, so search for a particularly warm location for drying.

Some flowers dry best in this upright position, but without the water as described above. Those with an umbel (a round, sturdy head of flowers on individual stems), such as dill and Queen-Anne's-lace, keep a better, more natural form with this method. Flowers which have a small spike of blooms, such as astilbe, lavender, liatris, and veronica, should be dried hanging upside down.

Other flowers will require the use of a drying agent, such as borax, white sand, corn meal, or silica gel. This last is the most expensive but is lighter in weight than sand and does not alter the form of the blooms as easily as a heavier drying medium could. There are a few popular "mixes," such as half borax and half sand, or half borax and half corn meal. Several good books available from the library or bookstore go into the various agents and methods in greater detail.

To dry plant material in the microwave, a drying agent is still necessary, but the total time required for drying is cut from days to minutes. The best way to determine what works is to experiment with several of these methods.

When a drying agent is used, flowers are usually cut with short stems and a wire stem is added. Do not wire the stems before drying if using the microwave. Place blooms face down in a flat box or other container which has a layer of drying agent in the bottom. Carefully pour more drying agent around and over each flower, taking care to retain the flower's natural form.

Silica gel is a lightweight, blue-and-white granular substance with a consistency similar to sugar and may be used over and over. As moisture is absorbed from the plant material, the blue color of some granules will fade away and the material takes on a pinkish white color. To restore their ability to absorb moisture, spread the crystals out in a thin layer in a shallow pan and place in a 300° oven to dry. When they have regained their original blue-and-white color, remove them from the oven. Place in a tightly covered container to cool. If the container is metal, it should be heated before the crystals are poured into it to prevent condensation which would be absorbed by the silica gel. When it has cooled, label the container and store in a warm, dry place.

A flat box is suitable for drying flowers and foliage in the microwave. Spread a layer of silica gel in the bottom of the box. Place short-stemmed blooms face up, taking care they do not touch one another. Sift or carefully pour silica gel around the blooms, retaining the natural form of the plant material. Cover with about an inch of silica gel, and place in the microwave oven. A microwave thermometer is helpful for determining the amount of time required; the middle temperature setting on the microwave is usually best. Titia Joosten's book, *Flower Drying with a Microwave Oven*, recommends a temperature of 150–170° F for most flowers. Set the timer for about two minutes. Remove the container and carefully tip off enough silica gel to expose the petal edges of a few flowers. If the petal edges are dry to the touch, re-cover them with the warm silica gel and allow the container to set until the drying agent is cool. This cooling period is very important. If petal edges are not dry, more drying time is required; re-cover with silica gel and allow another thirty seconds of drying time in the microwave, then test again.

When all petals test dry and the silica gel has cooled, slowly pour the material off and remove the dried flowers. Most of the drying agent will fall off; use a small, soft brush to clean away any that remains.

The only way to determine drying time is by experimentation as it will vary from one plant material to another, from year to year, from season to season, depending upon many things. When using a method other than the microwave, some flowers will dry adequately in a week; others may take from two to three weeks. After a week in the drying agent, carefully remove one bloom to determine if it is totally dry; if not, replace it and allow another five to seven days before retesting. If plant material is left in any drying agent for too long a period, it will lose most of its color. The texture will be adversely affected and petals will become very brittle.

All successfully dried plant material must be stored carefully to avoid damage. It is best to store dried material in a box that has a packet of drying agent inside, such as those sometimes found in medication bottles. Do not place flowers on top of one another as they are very fragile. Seal or tightly cover the boxes and store in a warm, dark, dry place.

The following list gives some of the most useful plant materials and recommended methods of drying them; it is not intended to be all-inclusive but simply a sampling of those most commonly dried.

Achillea (YARROW)
> Hang, or air-dry upright.

Agapanthus (includes LILY-OF-THE-NILE)
> Hang, or air-dry upright.

Ageratum
> Hang, or air-dry upright.

Allium (CHIVES; ORNAMENTAL GARLIC)
> Hang, or air-dry upright.

Anemone (WINDFLOWER)
> Microwave.

Aquilegia (COLUMBINE)
> Blooms: hang. Seed pods: hang, or dry in a dessicant.

Artemisia (SAGEBRUSH)
> Hang.

Artichoke
> Hang, or air-dry upright.

Asclepias tuberosa (BUTTERFLY WEED)
> Hang, dry in a dessicant, or microwave.

Astilbe (SPIREA)
> Hang, or microwave.

Bamboo
> Hang, or air-dry upright.

Baptisia australis (FALSE INDIGO)
> Seed pods: hang.

Calendula (includes POT MARIGOLD)
> Hang.

Calluna (SCOTCH HEATHER)
> Hang, or place upright in one inch of water; allow water to evaporate; do not replenish water.

Celosia (includes COCKSCOMB)
> Hang.

Centaurea (includes BACHELOR'S-BUTTON)
> Dry in a dessicant, or microwave.

Chrysanthemum
> Dry in a dessicant.

Daucus carota (QUEEN-ANNE'S-LACE)
> Dry in a dessicant, or air-dry upright.

Delphinium (LARKSPUR)
> Blooms: dry in a dessicant, or microwave. Seed pods: Hang.

Dianthus (PINK; includes CARNATION)
> Hang, or microwave.

Digitalis (FOXGLOVE)
> Seed pods: hang.

Echinops (GLOBE THISTLE)
> Hang, or air-dry upright.

Erica (HEATH)
> Hang, or place upright in one inch of water; allow water to evaporate; do not replenish water.

Eucalyptus
> Seed pods: hang.

Fuchsia
    Dry in a dessicant, or microwave.
Gaillardia (BLANKET FLOWER)
    Hang.
Gerbera (includes TRANSVAAL DAISY)
    Dry in a dessicant, or microwave.
Gomphrena (includes GLOBE AMARANTH)
    Hang, or air-dry upright.
Grains (oats, wheat, barley, etc.)
    Hang, or air-dry upright.
Grasses (ornamental or wild)
    Seed heads: pick before ripe; hang.
Gypsophila (includes BABY'S BREATH)
    Hang, or air-dry upright.
Helianthus (SUNFLOWER)
    Hang, or air-dry upright.
Helichrysum monstrosum (STRAWFLOWER)
    Hang, or air-dry upright.
Heuchera (includes CORALBELLS)
    Hang, dry in a dessicant, or microwave.
Hosta (PLAINTAIN LILY; FUNKIA)
    Blooms: dry in a dessicant, or microwave. Foliage: place upright in one inch of water; allow water to evaporate; do not replenish water.
Hydrangea
    Place upright in one inch of water; allow water to evaporate; do not replenish water.
Iris (includes BEARDED, DUTCH, SPANISH)
    Seed pods: hang, or air-dry upright.
Lavandula (LAVENDER)
    Hang.
Liatris (GAY-FEATHER)
    Hang, or dry in a dessicant.
Limonium (STATICE)
    Hang.
Lunaria (HONESTY; DOLLAR PLANT)
    Seed pods: hang, or air-dry upright; remove husks when dry.
Narcissus (DAFFODIL)
    Dry in a dessicant, or microwave.
Moluccella laevis (BELLS-OF-IRELAND)
    Pick when beginning to dry on plant; place upright in one inch of water; allow water to evaporate; do not replenish water.
Papaver (POPPY)
    Seed pods: Hang.
Physalis alkekengi (CHINESE-LANTERN)
    Hang.
Paeonia (PEONY)
    Dry in a dessicant.
Rosa (ROSE)
    Dry in a dessicant, or microwave.
Rumex (DOCK)
    Hang.

Salix (includes PUSSY WILLOW)
    Hang, or air-dry upright.
Strelitzia (BIRD-OF-PARADISE)
    Hang, or place upright in one inch of water; allow water to evaporate; do not
    replenish water.

As we shall see, many factors influence the selection of design components. There will be a close relationship between the form of the design, the container, the plant material, color, and the planned placement of the design. Each choice is dependent upon the others. The final setting of the design will have an impact on its form and color and will help to determine the basics of container and plant material. Whatever the first selection, each factor enters into the equation. Careful consideration of each component and its effect on the other components and the whole will ensure the success of the completed design.

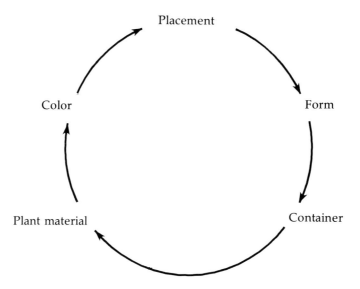

Diagram showing the interrelatedness of design components. The arranger can begin the selection process at any point on the circle but must go on to consider all related influences.

3 *Branching Out*

Decorative wood, one or more accessories, or a featured object adds distinction and expression to any arrangement. Time and again designers take advantage of one or more of these components to make a particular design more creative. One does not have a completely free hand with them, however. As with other elements, their use is governed by the principles of design and will require careful consideration and thoughtful selection. In flower shows, accessories and featured objects are permitted unless otherwise specified in the schedule.

DECORATIVE WOOD

By its very nature, a piece of wood is an original and often an antique: no two are exactly alike and most are very old. These are the very characteristics that lend a unique quality to designs. Less plant material is required in a design which includes decorative wood; this may be an advantage when flowers are scarce.

Weathered wood, driftwood, treated wood, and any number of other terms were used in the past to refer to a woody component, resulting in some confusion. This lack of clear definition often caused difficulties in flower show work. Nowadays, things are simplified, and the broader term *decorative wood* is used to encompass all types of wood. By it we mean any wood that has been waxed, varnished, painted, or treated in such a way that its surface quality and/or color has been changed; wood whose surface has been altered by the elements, in color, form, and/or texture; dried branches; sections of tree limbs or trunks; burls; cypress knees; and even some woody seed pods, usually tropical.

Decorative wood is useful in both Traditional and Creative flower arrangements, though perhaps the floral arranger working on Creative designs will find more ways to incorporate wood into a design. The key is to develop a seeing eye and recognize the potential in any type of material. Be especially sensitive to interesting forms, textures, and colors.

Decorative wood may be used as line material, container, abstract form, base, or background; it may even itself be a featured object. An unusual piece of wood is often found in Assemblages, Collages, Constructions, Mobiles, and other types of Creative designs, all of which will be covered in detail in chapter eight.

An interpretive design titled "Wildfire." Two pieces of decorative wood have been temporarily joined and painted black to depict the charred forest. Stems of orange-red gladiolus follow the lines of the wood, representing the flames that consume everything in their path.

Many different colors, forms, and textures occur in decorative wood in its natural state. Much depends upon the kind of wood, of course; fir differs from cedar, elm from oak, and so on. Where it is found and what has affected its surface qualities further individualize a piece; even charred wood, for instance, may have beautiful form, as well as unique color and texture.

Decorative wood can be found in the mountains and in the desert, along seashores, riverbeds, and lakeshores, in fields and woods, and in and around the ruins of old wooden buildings. For example, weathered barn boards may have a lovely color and texture. Mountain timberlines offer low, spare, wind-twisted branches. The desert yields sand-blasted, sun-bleached wood with a subtle silver patina. Ghostwood, ironwood, mesquite, and sage brush all grow into unusual forms.

Early spring is often the best time to scour the shores of man-made lakes, especially those created by dams, for uprooted trees or stumps. Roots which have been subjected to changing water levels often have beautiful form and gradations of texture. They can be sawed off while exposed and may prove useful in many ways. Wood found along lakes and rivers will likely be superior to that found on the beach as, under normal circumstances, it has been more gently shaped; wood that has been roughly tossed about by the regular action of ocean waves may be badly broken. Nevertheless, winter—or just after a storm—is usually the best time at the beach for turning up those pieces of wood that have held together, as well as other potentially useful items, such as dried plant material, seashells, pieces of beach glass, or perhaps a glass fishing float.

Whatever the body of water, the action of water upon wood and its bark changes and enriches its form, color, and texture. Boards and branches that have been subjected to this action over a long period of time have rounded edges, interesting form, and subdued color. They may be suitable for a base or provide an interesting background for an Assemblage on a panel or for a Collage.

Very small pieces of wood, water-tossed or not, may provide the material for an Assemblage on just such a panel. Burls or naturally hollowed pieces of tree limbs can sometimes be utilized as a container.

Whenever and wherever you collect wood, be sure not to trespass on private property. Take along clippers, gloves, and a small saw, and choose only those pieces that can be used without too much sanding, chiseling, carving, or other preparation. Unless one has the patience to spend many hours working on a single piece of wood, it is better to be selective at the outset. Professional sand-blasting is possible, but the expense can be prohibitive.

Only on rare occasions will wood be found that is ready to be used in an arrangement without cleaning or some other treatment. Regardless of where it has been collected, most wood will require hosing off to remove soil and insects. Scrub the wood with warm, soapy water and a stiff brush, and rinse well to remove soapy residue. If there are decayed areas or holes in the wood, the entire piece should be sprayed with an insecticide before it is taken into the house or garage.

When the wood is dry, examine it carefully. Use a small chisel or similar instrument to remove any wood that appears decayed. You may want to take advantage of the wide variety of small woodworking tools commonly available at hardware stores. Frequently, removing decayed wood impacts color by revealing a previously unexposed portion of wood; it will be necessary to treat this area in some way so that it again blends with the natural color surrounding it. Chalk, paint, and furniture or shoe polish are all effective.

A little sheen may be all that is needed to make some pieces more attractive. Simply rub the wood by hand with a soft cloth. If even more sheen is required, apply clear paste floor wax with a soft cloth, and rub until the desired effect is produced. Paste wax is also available in green, brown, or black and can augment or even change the existing color of a piece.

There are several other ways to change the color of wood. Many of the following methods are a matter of experimentation, with frequent checks in the process necessary to see when the desired color has been achieved. Diluted laundry bleach may be used to lighten wood; some enthusiasts use bleach at full strength to give wood a yellow-beige color. The wood must remain in the solution until the desired color effect is obtained; it will not continue to lighten once removed. It is therefore advisable to follow these procedures outdoors, as using chemicals that give off strong fumes in an enclosed area can be harmful.

Warm linseed oil can be rubbed onto wood and buffed with a soft cloth to darken the color and produce a soft, warm glow. The beautiful silver patina found in desert-weathered pieces often results when wood is left to bleach in the hot sun.

Painting is a less desirable method of changing the natural color of decorative wood for once applied there is no regaining the natural finish, and the grain is often obscured. However, when pieces of wood are to be attached to one another, it may be impossible to find pieces of the same color, and painting may be the only way to achieve the necessary uniformity. Sometimes wood from different types of trees may be made to match in color by spraying a little paint on a cloth and wiping the cloth over all surfaces. Interesting color effects may be obtained using two or more different colors of paint. For one effect, allow the first coat to dry, then overspray a very little of another color or two in a few places until the desired effect is achieved. Move the can rapidly over the surface to avoid overpainting; just a little paint may be all that is needed. For another effect, apply one coat and then another or two, allowing each to dry thoroughly before applying the next. Using a cloth saturated with a little turpentine, smudge off the layers of color in spots until you are pleased with the result. Wear rubber gloves, and work outdoors.

A paint with a flat finish often leaves wood with an undesirable, lifeless appearance. The finish of wood thus treated can be vastly improved by touching it up with a few swishes of glossy paint in the same color. Semi-gloss paint is a better initial selection, if available. Many arrangers continue to use only flat black, brown, or white to paint wood, but they would do well to add a bit of gloss and expand their palette. Other colors may add beauty and interest, or change the character of the wood in a dramatic way. Indeed, wood can be painted any color that is suitable for the purpose for which it is being prepared.

Most pieces of wood will require some alteration even if it is only to saw off a portion of the bottom, creating a flat plane for stability, or to attach a needleholder. Before making an alteration, consider the action very carefully. Look at the piece of wood from all angles: right side up, upside down, and from all sides. Some branches or other protrusions may need to be sawed off and discarded, or reattached at another spot.

Pieces of wood can be attached to one another in a number of ways. The least satisfactory method is the use of nails or screws, as they may either split the wood or not hold firmly. If this is the only available method, splitting can be prevented by drilling a hole of the proper size before using either a nail or a screw. Hot glue is sometimes used to attach pieces that are light in weight, but glue may later fail to hold.

The best method involves wooden dowels or metal rods. First, carve, chisel, or saw the two ends to be attached until a perfect fit is achieved. Pieces may be planed smooth at this juncture or be joined together in a more complicated way, like jigsaw puzzle pieces. Drill a hole at the proper angle in each piece to be fitted. Be sure the holes drilled are the proper size to allow for the insertion of the rod or dowel you have chosen. A tight fit is essential. Apply a little wood glue to one end of the dowel or rod. Insert the glued end into one piece of the wood. Apply glue to the protruding portion of the rod and position the remaining piece of wood over and onto it, making sure to adjust the two to obtain a neat joint. Allow the glue to dry before using the wood. Wood putty can be used to make a smoother joint if a perfect fit is impossible; however, it will be necessary to paint the entire piece to conceal the putty, which may not be desirable.

Sometimes storage or transportation of a large, jointed piece would be problematic. For example, a large piece of wood, for line, attached to another piece of wood functioning as a base can yield something quite unwieldy. It is better to join two such pieces only temporarily, so that they can be taken apart and reassembled with ease. In this case, the hole drilled in the base should be made very slightly larger than the rod or dowel, making for easy insertion and removal of the top piece. Use glue only on that part of the rod that will be inserted into the upright piece, where the smaller, snug-fitting hole has been drilled.

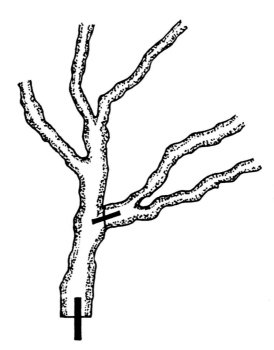

In this illustration, the branch on the right has been planed smooth and attached permanently to the main vertical piece using a dowel glued on both ends. At bottom, the dowel is glued only to the upright line of decorative wood, and the entire piece is ready for temporary attachment to a base.

Where wood is involved, mechanics may be difficult. Many otherwise-lovely designs have been ruined by unstable or untidy mechanics. Pieces that are small, well balanced, and light in weight can be controlled with a special needleholder made for the purpose, described in the previous chapter. The bottom plane of a dried branch may be prepared by cutting an X into it, allowing it to be impaled on even a regular needleholder. In Traditional designs, wood is often of a size and weight suitable for use with one of these methods.

In Creative designs, the wood is almost always much larger and heavier, and other methods of control will be necessary. For instance, a natural protrusion in the wood may allow the piece to be hung over the edge of the container. Sometimes the wood can be attached to the container with hot glue and removed later. Since each piece will present its own challenges, no one method will always be successful. Once again, simple experimentation is the best way to find a solution to each problem posed. Any method that is neat, unobtrusive, and functional is permissible.

Once properly joined and controlled, wood is nearly ready to take one of its many possible places in a design. Decorative wood may be used to make an abstract form by attaching it inside a frame. With the addition of a few flowers, the form of the wood becomes a design in itself or may be incorporated into a larger design. A few pieces of evergreen foliage or some dried flowers added to the framed form will make an attractive winter arrangement—especially welcome when fresh flowers are not readily available.

Lengths of branches, such as birch, may be attached to one another, resulting in beautiful Constructions, which require only the addition of a few flowers and a little foliage to complete the design. Eucalyptus bark which has been naturally shed may be slit and other pieces then inserted, creating another unusual Sculptural Form or Construction, or at the least, a most creative piece of line material. A large limb or section of a small tree trunk may be used as a container by hollowing out an area which would accommodate a small can with a needleholder, or some oasis. The shell of a burl may make a tray, as well as a container; add small pieces of decorative wood for feet or place the shell on a small wrought-iron stand. Raising wood makes it appear less visually heavy and more attractive, much as the stem of a compote adds grace to its form.

Wood that has good three-dimensional form may be the basis for a Sculptural Form design. A tall metal rod with a footed bottom will position the wood in space; this contributes to the overall sculptural feeling. Often such a stand can be obtained from a store that is going out of business or from a display house; welders or artists who work with metal could also fashion one.

For very large pieces, it is best to keep the center of gravity low. In this case, a shorter rod is inserted into a square wooden block with a finish and color similar to that of the decorative wood. If the wood is quite large, it can be drilled and placed on a rod in the manner described earlier, though with the heaviest pieces, it is better for the rod to remain glued to the solid base rather than to the wood. Whether the rod is permanently attached to the base or to the upright piece, this method is a smart choice as both the base and wood are almost certainly suitable for use in more than one arrangement.

ACCESSORIES

An accessory is anything added to a design other than plant material, container, base, background, or mechanics. Accessories are often included in designs and are meant to be noticed, of course, but only as the most subtle of supporting players; they must always remain subordinate to other elements in the arrangement. In Traditional designs, accessories are likely to be realistic figurines of birds, animals, and people, or an interesting object, such as a fan, book, or paperweight. In Creative designs, accessories are most often themselves abstracted forms or art objects.

To be legitimately included in a design, one or more accessories may serve any of several purposes. They may add interest, repeat a color or form, interpret a theme, or assist in establishing balance. Decorative wood is not considered an accessory unless it has been purposely shaped into an object, such as a carved bird.

An accessory may be placed on the table or base beside the design, on the lip of the container, or within the design in another manner. An accessory never provides the structural line of a design as an accessory is always subordinate.

FEATURED OBJECTS

A featured object, sometimes called a feature, is the dominant object in a design, yet it is always something other than plant material. Realistic (often religious) figurines or birds are often featured in Traditional designs. As might be expected, the objects featured in Creative floral designs are almost always stand-alone, abstracted art forms. Unlike the subordinate accessory, which one should properly be able to remove without significant harm to a design, a feature is centerstage. The design rests entirely upon it; take it away, and the integrated design is lost.

Do not let the semantics confuse you on this point. Every design has something that may be said to be featured or dominant, such as a certain color or type of plant material, but not all designs have a featured object. When a design is planned around a featured object, all colors and materials exist only to support its central presence in the design.

4 Aesthetically Speaking: The Elements and Principles of Design

The elements and principles of design apply to every art form, flower arranging included. The elements are the components that make up the design; the principles are the ways in which the elements are combined. Taken together, they might be compared to a recipe in a cookbook. The elements of design—color, light, space, line, form, pattern, texture, and size—are the ingredients. The principles of design—balance, dominance, contrast, rhythm, proportion, and scale—are the directions, telling one how to prepare and mix the ingredients to achieve an artful result. In the previous chapters we assembled the essential equipment of flower arranging; we now turn to the concepts behind the art of arrangement itself.

THE ELEMENTS OF DESIGN

It is difficult to discuss any one of the elements without touching on the others, such is their interrelatedness. A change in one may be necessary to achieve or strengthen an effect in another. Color is the element which first attracts us in a design. It is so important a visual and emotional element and so far-reaching in its effects, it merits its own chapter—the next—and will require more study than any of the others, which are considered here in turn.

Light

Light must be present to view a design, of course, but in its many gradations and types, it also affects how well a design comes across and exerts a strong influence on both color and texture. Light may be either natural (sunlight) or artificial (manufactured). The varying intensity of natural light affects the perceived color of an object. Consider the diffused light of a foggy day; everything looks more delicate in such light. The same colors under a bright, tropical sun will be more vivid and seem to glow. By observing the brightest flowers in the garden as the sun begins to set, this phenomenon is clearly illustrated. Colors will gradually change and fade away until little color remains as darkness approaches. It is interesting to note which colors fade away first and which are the last that can be identified.

Artificial lighting may be incandescent or fluorescent, black or strobe, floodlight or spotlight. Each of these has a different effect on flower arrangements, with the color palette affected more than any other element. Incandescent lights have a yellow undertone; fluorescent lights give a bluish green cast. Both may adversely affect the color of plant material. Most homes use either incandescent or fluorescent lighting—or a combination of the two—and one must select the colors for an arrangement meant for the home accordingly. When a flower that was bright and appealing outdoors seems to change color, becoming dull and lifeless indoors, it is the switch from natural to artificial light that has caused the problem.

Simply stated, when light falls on a surface, some light rays are absorbed and others are reflected. The reflected light rays are the color perceived by the viewer. A red rose absorbs all but red light rays, which color is reflected from its surface. Since incandescent light produces more yellow rays, there are fewer blue rays to be reflected from the surface. For this reason, blue flowers appear grayish green and are lost in a design displayed under incandescent light. Red, yellow, and yellow-green are intensified, however. The bluish green cast of fluorescent lighting intensifies blues and greens, but warm hues are grayed by it.

When creating a design for a public building or flower show, the wise arranger begins by learning the type of lighting to be used in the area where the design will be staged. Only then can the proper selection of plant material be made. It is disappointing to create a lovely design in an exciting color combination only to have the effect ruined when the lights are turned on or the design is placed in its intended site. The best learning method is still that of trial and error: cut samples of various colors of plant material and view them under different types of light to determine how they are changed and which remain effective.

In some public buildings or flower shows, special lighting may be permitted or even required, and the arranger is usually expected to provide the means. The light source may be placed in front of, behind, above, below, or to either or both sides of the design; each placement yields a different effect. Floodlights illuminate the entire design; spotlights throw focus on a single aspect of it. Colored bulbs may be used to create a special mood. The type and direction of light affects depth of form. Textures may be made to appear rougher or smoother; form may be enhanced; shadows created. Side lighting casts shadows on the side opposite the light source; lights from above create shadows beneath an object; front lighting alone gives the appearance of a lack of depth in the design. A form may be enhanced by a spotlight aimed directly on it, making it more dominant, or strengthened by the strong shadows cast behind it. Plant material may even be treated with fluorescent paint so that it glows under a black light. The advanced flower arranger will find experimenting with the effects of various lighting techniques a fascinating study.

Space

Space is not a void, but rather an important design element. For the flower arranger, it includes not only the space within the design itself, but also the spatial dimensions of a design's final location, including the wall behind it. This type of site-specific space is one over which the arranger has little control unless the design is meant for the home, in which case furniture may be moved or another spot found for the design. In a flower show, the schedule determines the total space allowed for each exhibit.

The spaces within the plant material and other components are alterable on a limited scale; the spaces between leaves on a stem, for example, may be increased by some judicious pruning. The plant material itself, the container, and base are all opportunities for control by choice. An arranger may choose an urn with open handles and a slender stem for its inherent space over a more dense, straight-up-and-down cylinder. The base may be either a solid block or one elevated by legs, leaving open space beneath it. As to plant material, flowers such as tulips and lilies have three-dimensional, or volumetric, space within the open bloom, whereas there is little space left by the density of a football chrysanthemum, which is a solid form fully occupying its space.

The spaces created within a design are under the complete control of the arranger. As the overall design inevitably has depth of form, the spaces created within it will have depth or volumetric space as well. In addition to depth, space may be said to have size, form, color, and texture. The size or amount of space will vary and may be very large, very small, or somewhere in between. The form of space depends in great measure upon the placement of the design components and may be geometric or free-form, vertical or horizontal, open or enclosed. The color and texture of space is determined by the background, or what is seen behind the space. In the home, this may be an expanse of plain painted wall, drapes, wallpaper, or paneling. In a flower show, the background or niche is usually covered with solid-colored fabric in Traditional design classes; this may vary in Creative design classes.

Space as such has become especially important in Creative design. Components may be used by the arranger in such a way that space is creatively formed, divided, penetrated, and organized by the skillful placement of lines and forms; it is not something merely "left over" or filled. In Traditional designs, space is simply occupied by form. In Creative designs, space—even that which is left empty—is an inherent and vital part of the whole. To put it another way, Creative designs are designs *of* space, rather than designs *in* space.

Line

Line is the basic foundation of all design, and it is line which creates the visual framework in floral design. Line determines the eye's visual path, the natural and logical sequence which the eye follows over a design, and so greatly affects the principle of rhythm. The eye moves swiftly along straight, smooth-flowing, uninterrupted lines, in a fast, staccato manner over sharp angles, and more slowly along gently curving lines.

Pure line has only one dimension: length. In flower arranging, length is the primary dimension. Though most linear material has some width as well, it will almost always be far less than the length. Grasses have little width, yucca and phormium a bit more, and a spike of gladiolus still more, but nevertheless width remains secondary to length.

Line, however lengthy, may be further described as long or short, thick or thin, delicate or bold, straight or curved. And a line's direction contributes to the mood of a design. Vertical lines appear to be uplifting or inspirational; lines which curve up are exciting; those that curve down may appear lifeless or wilted. Horizontal lines seem to be quiet, at rest, and are therefore relaxing; a dynamic zig-zag line is reminiscent of lightning and swift movement; oblique lines appear to be on the move and are exciting to view.

Form

Form is three-dimensional, contrasted with shape, which has only two dimensions. A lemon has form; a picture of that same lemon has only shape. Three-dimensional geometric forms based on the cone, sphere, cube, and cylinder are basic to all floral design. Designs are created through the manipulation of these geometric forms. In Traditional designs, the form—whether triangular, vertical, spherical, diagonal, horizontal, spiral, or S-curve—is easily identified. Here manipulation involves only the reduction of a form to one of its parts; for instance, a crescent form is used rather than the whole sphere. The same geometric forms are used in Creative designs, but since manipulation is more dramatic or extreme, the viewer may find them more difficult to identify. Here the forms may be elongated, compressed, divided, or combined.

There are two types of form, open and closed. An open form has space between its parts and appears lighter in weight than a closed form of the same size and color. A lily, for instance, is an open form; there is space within the spreading petals of the flower. A carnation is a closed form; solid and compact, with little space between the petals, it will appear heavier than an open form of the same size. The form of the entire design may also be either open or closed. A Line design is an open form; a Traditional Mass design has closed form.

Depth of form is the critical third dimension in floral design. It may be obtained through a naturalistic placement of materials, that is, arranging some material in profile and overlapping others. Incorporating diagonal thrust and movement and planning for areas of tension contributes to the spatial illusion. The use of advancing and receding colors and transparent forms will also add to the perceived depth of a design.

Round forms, such as incurved chrysanthemums, are regular forms which attract the eye but do not hold it. Irregular forms hold the eye longer as it takes longer to view them. Orchids, anthuriums, and birds-of-paradise are always irregular forms. Other blooms, like lilies or daffodils, are regular forms in reality but appear irregular when viewed from the side, making them irregular forms in practice.

Pattern

Pattern is present on two levels. In plant material, it is the placement of petals, stems, and foliage as found in nature, sometimes orderly, sometimes not. For example, the needles on a pine branch have a very regular pattern, but the pattern of individual stems on that same branch may be very uneven. In the completed design, pattern is created by the arrangement of solids, spaces, and color within the design.

The pattern formed by the petals in a rose is concentric and varies only in the size of the spaces between the petals which become ever smaller and closer together as they near the center. The pattern of a spike of gladiolus is very regular with each floret symmetrically in place, tapering from open florets at the bottom to tight buds at the top. Several spikes of gladiolus may form another pattern entirely at the design level; the effect is up to the designer. If each is placed in an upright position, close together, the result is a vertical pattern which closely echoes the pattern of the spike. If placed with the tips widely spaced, a fan-shaped pattern is the result. Two spikes placed close together in an upright position with a third placed toward the horizontal will form yet another pattern. The possibilities are endless.

The color pattern within plant material may be provided by the variegation of foliage, different-colored margins on the flowers, or the placement of blooms along a branch. The arrangement of colors within the design determines the color pattern and establishes color rhythm. In summary, pattern is found at one level within the components themselves, but pattern is further developed by the arrangement of these same components into a design having a pattern of its own.

Texture

Texture is the surface quality of an object and may be rough or smooth, hard or soft, glossy or dull, coarse or fine. The viewer has both an emotional and a visual reaction to texture. One may be repelled by the rough, spiny texture of barrel cactus or attracted to the rich, luxurious texture of lamb's-ears. Experience teaches us that anything velvety is smooth and pleasant to the touch while the spines on the cactus may cause pain. Once experienced, we either reach out to touch or draw away from the item because of its apparent texture. The word "apparent" is used as we may be fooled by appearance. For example, most pines have rough, bristly needles, yet the Japanese white pine has needles that are extremely soft and pleasing to the touch.

Texture also relates to form, size, and color. A large form with rough or coarse texture is visually broken into smaller planes, making the large form appear smaller in size. A rough texture makes the same form appear heavier. Smooth or shiny surfaces reflect light from a single area making the form appear larger yet lighter and the color stronger. Conversely, rough textures make color appear weaker.

A variety of textures adds interest to a design while a sameness of texture becomes monotonous. Textural contrasts add interest to flower arrangements, but one texture must be dominant; too much texture gives a fussy effect. Rough textures cause the eye to move slowly and are useful where the designer wishes to draw attention; smooth textures allow for rapid eye movement.

Size

Though each component has both visual and actual dimensions, size as it relates to design is only concerned with the visual or apparent. Unlike actual size, visual size varies with the distance from the viewer, in comparison to other objects viewed simultaneously, and according to the color and texture of the component. A large object seen from far away is apparently small in size; when a small object is seen next to a large object, the small object appears smaller and the larger object even larger; advancing hues—those in which highly visible colors dominate—and white or very light values make an object appear larger in size. As we have said, a coarse texture, by breaking up the light reflections, makes an object appear smaller in size. Smooth, shiny textures make an object visually larger in size.

Actual size may be small and delicate or large and bold, but the importance of a form in a design is more dependent upon its visual size. Of course, a very large chrysanthemum will always be a more important form than a smaller one, whatever the design. The smaller mum might be very lovely on a bedside table but would be totally insignificant on a church altar. Size is closely related to the design principles of proportion and scale.

This Creative design offers a lesson in the importance of component compatibility. The Queen-Anne's-lace blooms are too small in size and too delicate in both form and color for the strong line and visually heavy container. On the positive side, the loops and twists of the wisteria vine create enclosed spaces which successfully repeat those found in the container.

Here, 'Stargazer' lilies have replaced the Queen-Anne's-lace. Their color, form, and size work well in concert with the vine, and they are arranged to follow the line created by the vine, leaving the enclosed spaces visible.

THE PRINCIPLES OF DESIGN

The principles of design—balance, dominance, contrast, rhythm, proportion, and scale—are the plan by which the elements of design are organized. How the elements of design are arranged to meet the principles of design is the measure of success in flower arranging.

Balance

Balance is visual, the impression of stability and equilibrium. Physical or actual balance by weight is affected by gravity and may not be visual balance. Balance is generally described as being of two types, symmetrical and asymmetrical. Symmetrical balance, or formal balance, requires a repetition of elements on both sides of the axis with the two sides as nearly alike as possible. An axis is one or more central lines (real or imaginary) around which an artistic form is organized or composed; it is always vertical and will be through the middle or focal area of a Traditional design.

Placement of individual pieces of plant material will either support or destroy visual and physical balance. The visual weight of plant material is determined by size, color, and texture. Small plant material, light in color value, is light in visual weight as well and is usually placed towards the top and the outer periphery of the design. As plant material is placed lower and nearer the center of the design, it should gradually become larger in size and darker or brighter in color. Material which is largest in size and darkest or brightest in color should be closest to the container and nearest to the central axis. In Traditional designs with symmetrical balance, the longest vertical line is placed over the center of the container or axis. If this line is curved, its tip should end directly over the axis for visual stability.

Asymmetrical, or informal, balance is the balancing of different elements. The elements on the two sides of the axis will be different but will have equal visual weight. The axis need not be through the middle of the container in a design which is asymmetrically balanced. If the container has a stem—a compote, for example—the axis has been established by the stem of the container. A design in a cylinder will usually have an established axis through the middle of the container; however, a flat, oblong container may have the axis at any place determined by the arranger. Here, balance is obtained through counterbalance. Larger plant material placed near the axis is counterbalanced by longer lines of lighter weight further from the axis on the opposite side.

Since elements have differing visual weight, it is important to remember that bold, dense forms, large sizes, dark colors, and coarse textures have greater visual weight than their opposites. Forms have more weight than enclosed space, and open spaces are visually very light in weight.

Visual balance also depends upon placement. A form of the same size and color used higher or further away from the axis will appear heavier than the same form used lower in the design and closer to the axis. By placing large, dark, coarse-textured plant material just above the container, the arranger establishes visual stability. Too much weight placed low in the design can make the design bottom-heavy, however. Since space has less weight than form, space provided under the container by a footed base will make the design appear less heavy and not so earthbound.

A black metal container has been combined with several rough-textured pieces of decorative wood sprayed black. Two stems of pink lilies complement the form, but this Creative design is a bit out of balance on the lower right.

Balance has been improved by the addition of foliage. The leaf extending outward on the bottom right solves the problem.

Balance is necessary from side to side and front to back. A design lacking side-to-side balance appears unstable. A design lacking front-to-back balance appears flattened or "cut off" in the back. Greater height may be required to balance a too-heavy container and/or base; more plant material may be needed in the back of the design to balance that in front; a smaller form further from the axis may be necessary to balance a larger one close to the axis.

Static balance may be found in either symmetrical or asymmetrical balance and is achieved by equal actual or visual balance on either side of the axis exerting equal force. Static balance is most often found in Traditional designs and is the least interesting kind of balance. Finding nothing of great contrast or opposition, the eye moves quickly through the design.

Dynamic balance is achieved through the use of contrasting or opposing elements, such as opposing sizes or directions, contrasting forms, color values, or textures. These opposing or contrasting elements create a tension which translates as interest, and as a result, the eye moves more slowly through the design. Dynamic balance is the hallmark of Creative designs.

Yet another type of balance involves color. In general, a small amount of full-intensity color is balanced by a larger amount of a duller color; however, the proportion of color fields affects balance. Too large an area of dull color cannot be balanced by too small an area of a bright color. In Creative designs, especially Abstract, two or more hues of full intensity may be counterbalanced to create areas of equated interest. The usual tack of balancing intense color against dull color may be undesirable in Abstract designs.

Dominance

Dominance is the greater force of one element over others. It goes hand in hand with subordination. There may be more of one color than another; more round forms than spike forms; more straight lines than curved. Dominance should be evident immediately; one should not have to search for it. In Traditional flower arrangements, the container is always subordinate to the plant material; this is not always true of Creative designs.

Bold forms, bright colors, or repeated elements will help achieve dominance in a design. There are degrees of and limits to what the element of repetition can accomplish, however. Several long lines moving in the same direction placed close together will be more dominant than the same lines widely spaced. Many stems of asparagus fern might be used along with one large, bright red rose, but no amount of asparagus fern will ever dominate the rose. Repetition alone does not necessarily create dominance.

Contrast

Contrast is achieved by the juxtapositioning of different or unlike elements. It exists only as one element or dimension is compared to a related one. With color, bright contrasts with pale; with length, long contrasts with short; with texture, smooth contrasts with rough; with form, round contrasts with spiked.

Contrast adds interest to a design but must be used sparingly as too much contrast divides attention and leads to confusion. The contrast of opposites creates an illusion which strengthens the strong and weakens the weak. When a strong color is contrasted with a weak color, the strong color will appear stronger and more important while the weak color appears even weaker and less important. Both colors will attract more attention when contrasted with the other than either would attract alone.

Contrast of color also helps to define form. A bright red rose against a red background is difficult to distinguish. Position the same bright rose against a white background and the form becomes clear. One leaf on a maple tree is simply a part of a large, green, textured mass—until the leaf is singled out and placed against a contrasting color.

Rhythm

Rhythm suggests timing and motion; it is rhythm that leads the eye through a design and determines the direction and duration of the trip. Rhythm is achieved through repetition, line, and gradation. Repetition of a line direction, form, or color will produce rhythm. Line creates rhythm as the eye is drawn along its length. Several straight lines repeated in an upward thrust will lead the eye in an upward direction; a series of small curves creates another type of rhythm.

Gradation implies a slow progression from large to small sizes, dark to light colors, coarse to fine textures; each will coax the eye through a design. Gradation in sizes—from large at the base of the design, gradually changing to small-sized plant material at the top—will establish rhythm or eye movement. Rhythm can be smooth and flowing, fast or slow, jarring and syncopated, gradual or abrupt. Designs without rhythm will not move us.

Proportion

Proportion is the relation of the size of areas and amounts to each other and the whole. All measurement is relative. Only when one element is considered in relation to another is it found to be too long, too short, too tall, or too wide. Every form has proportion as every form has length, width, and depth. Proportion is the amount of plant material in relation to the container; the size of the design as it relates to the background; the amount of round forms in relation to spike forms; or the amount of bright colors to dull. It is the relative area or volume of form or space, or the relative length of one line to another.

Equal amounts or equal dimensions are uninteresting. The Golden Mean is a ratio of parts expressed in numbers, 1:1.6, which has long been considered the ideal proportion. In Traditional Early 20th-Century American designs, this is borne out by the suggested ratio of line material being at least one-and-one-half times the height or diameter of the container. Creative designers are likely to use line material that is four or more times the height or diameter of the container. Arrangers have gradually become accustomed to these greater dimensions and find them, too, pleasing.

Scale

Scale is the size of one object in relation to another. Scale applies only to size, as the size of one flower to another; the size of one flower to the container; the size of an accessory to the container or to one flower. When there is too much difference in the size of one component as it relates to another they are said to be out of scale, as the small chrysanthemum was not suited to the size of the altar.

Proper size relationships are essential. In the design on the left, although the yellow roses are in striking contrast to the black vine and container, they are out of scale with both the container and the foliage. In the version on the right, lilies have replaced the too-small roses and all components are now in scale. The container in this pair of designs was fashioned from downspout in the manner described in chapter two.

All this may seem confusing to the beginner; however, if one remembers that the physical components of a design contain the elements, and that they are tangible, it will be helpful. Plant material, for example, is one of the components of design and has color from reflected light, occupies space, and has visual line, form, texture, and size. We can touch the elements. The principles of design are intangible; they are the manner in which we arrange components to obtain proper and pleasing balance, dominance, contrast, rhythm, proportion, and scale. As one actually works with the elements and principles, they will become more easily understood and applied.

5 *The Color Whirl*

The study of color is a fascinating one, and understanding color is essential to floral design. The ability to accurately describe a desired color, to understand the effect of one color on another, and to anticipate how emotions are affected by certain colors can be a distinct advantage in flower arranging and beyond.

THE EFFECTS OF COLOR

In recent years, scientific studies have documented the many ways color can affect us. Industrial designers have taken the findings to heart: hospitals and schools make use of quiet, calming colors to encourage patients or students to remain calm and relaxed; fast-food restaurants do just the opposite, so that each seat in the limited space of the dining area will be quickly vacated by the last paying customer to make room for the next. Manufacturers package their products in colors meant to attract the eye of the consumer; in this case, whether the product is edible or not will have the final bearing on what is considered attractive, so that what is appropriate for a can of tomatoes is inappropriate for a beauty product or a box of detergent.

On a more personal level, a very popular book in the '80s was devoted to determining the colors most flattering to those having certain skin, hair, and eye coloring. Often a favorite color was found to be entirely wrong for an individual. As a result of the wide currency of this new notion, people became more aware of the importance of color and its influence on daily life. It was a simple matter to carry this color study one step further into interior design.

Color refers to an objective visual sensation; it is the response of vision to the wavelength of light reflected from a particular surface. Color begins with light as is easily seen in a rainbow or the colors reflected on a wall when sunlight strikes a prism. There is little color where there is little light; when light is strong, color is more intense.

Color is never seen alone; it is always seen in relation to the colors surrounding it. Local color is the color that would be seen if an object could be removed from all outside influence. The wall, background, niche, or other objects seen at the same time affect local color. The light source and amount will also affect the perceived color. Atmospheric color is what we perceive as a result of such outside influences. Neighboring colors may subdue one color and enhance another; color may be picked up from one object and reflected onto another. It is almost impossible to determine local color. Only if an object could be placed inside a completely white room, with perfect white light, would it be possible to determine local color. How color is seen and how it affects both arranger and viewer will influence its use in floral design.

The appeal of color is subjective as well; it affects each individual in a special, often unaccountable way. One may immediately like or dislike a color, be drawn to it or repelled by it, feel warmer or cooler, more calm or more excited. Some individuals may actually feel ill when exposed to a specific color and, whether flattering or not, may simply feel uncomfortable wearing or even being around it.

Other sometimes equally emotional associations may be attached to color. Certain combinations may have special meaning to a group or culture; for example, red, white, and blue mean one thing on the Fourth of July and another on Bastille Day. Others represent sports franchises or even political movements. Colors are associated with a specific season of the year; some are clearly springlike while others seem suitable only in winter. A particular holiday may be invoked, such as red and white for Valentine's Day, or a specific emotion, culturally determined, such as black for mourning in the United States. The association may even be based on a uniquely personal experience; however, the following, though sometimes conflicting, are considered universals.

yellow: The sun, sunshine, spring, cheerfulness, youth, wealth, luminosity, deceit, cowardice.

red: Danger, passion, excitement, fire, courage, aggression, hatred, heat, the devil.

blue: Peace, tranquility, sea, sky, water, cold, space, fidelity, cleanliness, depression, loneliness.

orange: Autumn, energy, warmth, vitality, strength, dullness, action.

green: Youth, envy, nature, rest, faith, hope, immaturity, springtime, immortality.

violet: Luxury, royalty, richness, solemnity, splendor, dignity, primness, fantasy, wisdom.

black: Depression, grief, darkness, sophistication, piracy, evil, magic, solemnity, severity.

gray: Twilight, restraint, dullness, old age, dignity, passivity, melancholy.

white: Purity, chastity, innocence, truth, coldness, light, serenity, cleanliness, honesty.

Color sets the tone of the arrangement and impacts all other elements in the design, as seen in the previous chapter. Color defines form, space, and line, establishes pattern, and affects texture. So strongly is the viewer influenced by color, it may even mask design faults; many designers take black-and-white as well as color photographs of an arrangement in order to uncover flaws they might not otherwise see.

Color also produces many other design effects. Red, orange, and yellow (associated with fire) are often referred to as warm colors. Bright and stimulating, they are considered to be holding, or advancing, colors. Blue, green, and violet (associated with water and ice) are often referred to as cool colors. Peaceful and tranquil, they are known as releasing, or retreating, colors. These qualities vary when white, gray, or black is added to a color. For instance, red with the addition of black goes from bright and exciting to dull and uninteresting. Stimulating colors draw the eye and hold it; releasing colors allow the eye to move more rapidly over a design. Skillful placement of color in floral designs will hold the eye where scrutiny is desired. Retreating colors are better used where the eye does not need to be drawn or held. Pure yellow is the most advancing color while blue seems furthest away, thus adding to the appearance of depth.

COLOR SYSTEMS AND LANGUAGE

Several color systems are utilized in the arts. The pigment system is the most common, holding that there are three basic or primary colors: yellow, blue, and red. In theory, all other colors can be obtained by mixing these colors. It is obvious that the artist whose medium is plant material cannot mix colors as a painter would; however, a basic understanding of colors and how they can relate to one another is helpful.

If one is mixing pure colors, equal amounts of red and yellow produce orange; equal amounts of yellow and blue produce green; and equal amounts of blue and red produce violet. These colors—orange, green, and violet—are secondary colors. There are additional colors which lie between the primary and secondary colors, known as intermediate colors. Blue-green falls between blue (a primary color) and green (a secondary color); yellow-orange between yellow (a primary color) and orange (a secondary color); blue-violet between blue (a primary color) and violet (a secondary color). There are many other variations, depending upon the amount of each color used. Neutral, or achromatic, colors are black, gray (a mixture of black and white), and white. By their addition to primary or secondary colors, many other colors are produced.

Color has three physical qualities or dimensions that must be considered in any artistic endeavor. The dimensions are hue, value, and intensity (sometimes called chroma).

Hue is the specific or family name of a color which distinguishes one color from another. The terms *color* and *hue* are used interchangeably. Hue (or color) may be red, yellow, blue, orange, green, blue-green, blue-violet, and so on.

Value is the lightness or darkness of a hue. A tint is a light value, the result of adding white. A shade is a dark value, the result of adding black. A red to which black has been added would be a shade of red. It is incorrect to call pink a "shade of pink"; it is actually a tint of red.

Intensity, or chroma, is the strength or purity of a hue. When gray or the hue's complement is added, the result is a tone. The degree of intensity is determined by the amount of gray or complement added. Intensity is lost as a color comes closer to gray; the more graying, the less the intensity. Full chroma or full intensity colors may be described as pure, intense, or strong; color in which the intensity has been diminished may be described as diluted, dull, or weak.

There are several useful guides to color, among them the color circle, the color wheel, and the color triangle. The color circle is composed of pure hues in their natural order as found in the color spectrum along with intermediate hues. The progression of these primary, secondary, and intermediate colors is as follows: yellow, yellow-orange, orange, red-orange, red, red-violet, violet, blue-violet, blue, blue-green, green, and yellow-green.

A color wheel is an augmented color circle, expanded to show many gradations of tints and shades ranging from the pure hue in the middle of each spoke toward black (shades) in the center and white (tints) on the outside.

The color triangle is made from one color with all its possible modifications from light values (tints) to white; from middle values (tones) to gray; and from dark values (shades) to black.

When choosing color, whether for a flower arrangement, a clothing ensemble, or to paint the house, the stronger the color, the less should be incorporated into the scheme. When using a dull or weak color, a larger amount may be used successfully. This is sometimes called the "law of color area," or color balance. In general, small amounts of strong color will visually balance large areas of a weak color; however, the proportion of each is important. Too large a field of dull color cannot be balanced by too small a field of a bright hue, as we saw in the previous chapter. Pleasing proportions of each are required for proper color balance.

Designs also have color pattern, rhythm, and balance. Repetition, variation, and the direction of color placement within a design provide the pattern and create the rhythmic flow of a design. Color balance builds on established pattern and rhythm with the addition of contrast and proportion. The repetition of one color with its variations provides contrast, and skillful placement of the color gives direction or rhythm to the design. The amount of colors and variation will provide color proportion, whether poor or pleasing.

As was the case in mixing hues, specific color harmonies are more difficult to achieve with living plant material than with paint and crayons. The visual artist creates his palette, but the floral designer is limited not only to the colors, but often to the combinations provided by nature. Despite the many possible combinations we are about to consider and with a nod to personal taste, the overriding concern in the home will always be to take into account the existing color scheme before choosing plant material for an arrangement.

COLOR HARMONIES AND SCHEMES

In all color harmonies, neither the designer nor the judge should be overly concerned with small or minute amounts of an unharmonious color. Stems are most often green, or brown with a greenish cast; flowers may have a small amount of yellow in their centers. These colors are a part of nature's plan, and such small inclusions should not be penalized.

Colors that relate to one another, whether analogously or monochromatically, yield the most visually satisfying harmonies. Analogous colors are those that lie next to one another on the color wheel, such as yellow, yellow-green, and green. Pure hues, tints, tones, and shades of these colors might be included in the color harmony. No more than one primary color or one-third of the colors on the wheel—but no fewer than three colors total—should be included. Allow one hue to be dominant, moving progressively from that hue to its neighboring colors, with no skips along the way. In flower shows, the container and the background or niche should be one of the related hues.

Monochromatic color harmonies are those that include tints, shades, and tones of one hue. If yellow were to be selected, only plant material in tints, tones, and shades of yellow would be included in the design. Such a monochromatic choice can become dull and uninteresting as there is less room for contrast than in

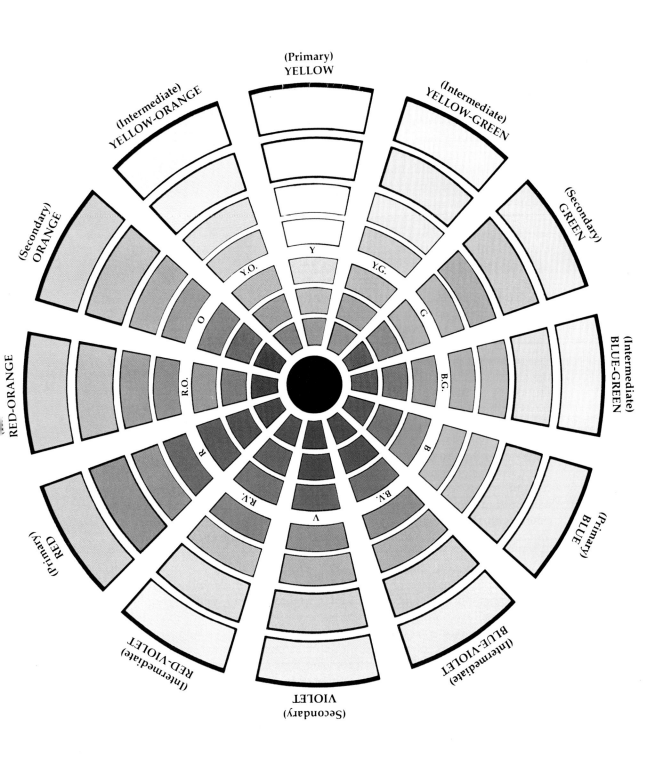

(Primary) YELLOW

(Intermediate) YELLOW-ORANGE

(Intermediate) YELLOW-GREEN

(Secondary) ORANGE

(Secondary) GREEN

RED-ORANGE

(Intermediate) BLUE-GREEN

(Primary) RED

(Primary) BLUE

(Intermediate) RED-VIOLET

(Intermediate) BLUE-VIOLET

(Secondary) VIOLET

Y
Y.O.
Y.G.
O
G
R.O.
B.G.
R
B
R.V.
B.V.
V

Color wheel

other color schemes. Monotony can be avoided by varying textures, sizes, and forms, though one each of the several textures, sizes, and forms should dominate. Wide steps between the color values also add interest. Monochromatic color harmonies are pleasing because they move in an orderly fashion from light to dark values.

Contrasting color schemes may be contrasts of color or value. Contrasting colors are complementary, such as red and green, yellow and violet, and orange and blue. The complement of each color is its direct opposite on the color wheel. There may also be complements of intermediate hues, such as yellow-green and red-violet, blue-green and red-orange, or blue-violet and yellow-orange. Contrasts of value may be from a tint to a shade: very light pink contrasted with a very dark shade of red. Black and white are the extremes of value contrast and very effective when used together. A harmony based on contrast is often very dramatic.

One of the keys to success in strict color harmonies is to include one of the selected colors in the container and the background as well as in the plant material. This repetition of color unifies the design; it is not an occasion to introduce contrast. If red roses are used in a green container, the container repeats the green color of their foliage unifying the design. If orange marigolds are arranged in a blue container, there is no unity, only sudden contrast. Those same orange marigolds arranged with a small number of blue flowers in a brown container would unify the design as brown is a very dark value of orange.

Dominance and contrast play important roles in color harmonies. The designer must avoid an even division of color by letting one color dominate and the others contrast in amount, value, and intensity. Nature has a masterful hand in the use of dominance and contrast. For example, the green foliage of holly contrasts strikingly with the red berries; in a variegated hosta leaf, green dominates the contrasting white or cream.

Split complements are yet another color scheme, but one that uses three hues rather than two. One hue is selected, and instead of using its direct complement, the designer uses the colors that lie on either side of that complement. The red and green contrasting harmony mentioned earlier would now become one using red in combination with yellow-green and blue-green; blue would be combined with red-orange and yellow-orange; or yellow combined with blue-violet and red-violet. The three hues are used in varying amounts and intensities. If red at full intensity is the dominant color, it would be combined with lesser amounts of yellow-green and blue-green of different intensities.

Another color harmony is a triad composed of three colors equidistant from one another on the color wheel, such as red-orange, yellow-green, and blue-violet, or yellow, blue, and red. The same general guidelines of varying amounts and intensities apply as in other harmonies.

Polychromy is the art of using many strong colors in harmonious combination, producing gay, carnival effects. The best examples of polychromatic color harmonies in floral art are the paintings of many of the Old Masters. In horticulture, a living example is the typical English garden and all its parts. Here many colors are combined, harmonized within a plot perhaps but not from grouping to grouping, separated and held together at once by colors—green, gray, or white—which work well with all, thus unifying the garden. This same theory applies to floral design: sections of bright hues may be separated by white, gray, or green—or simply by space in Creative designs.

This is not a totally new concept. Arrangers have combined many colors in

The quality of luster at work in a design. The pure yellow hue of the lilies and line material
is in vivid contrast to the dark blue of the background, appearing almost fluorescent
against it. The line material is nautical tow rope inserted with a stiff, heavy wire, making it
pliable yet free-standing.

Traditional designs in the past, but usually one color was dominant, and many values of that one color were used. In polychromatic designs, all colors, except for the unifying hues, are strong in value.

In Creative designs, varying color schemes are used without giving them much thought. One aims instead at communicating a mood or concept: harmony, discord, excitement. To deliberately try to work out a specific color harmony in a Creative design is a good exercise for study groups. These rather difficult assignments are the ones which stretch the mind and imagination but are rarely suitable for flower show schedules.

Additional color harmonies might include luster, iridescence, or luminosity. In his book, *Creative Color*, Faber Birren states that all three are "quite similar in visual phenomena." It is this subtlety that makes them intriguing study topics for the floral artist. It is a simple matter to incorporate one of these qualities into an existing harmony scheme.

The dictionary describes luster as "brilliance, brightness, or sheen." A large field of dark color contrasted with very small amounts of pure, intense hue will make those small areas dramatically brilliant in comparison, appearing even brighter than normal—an effect that is not lost on jewelers as they arrange their window displays! Designing against a dark background of black, navy, maroon, or brown is the first step. Small amounts of these dark colors may also be included in the flower arrangement. Plant material in pure hues will stand out against such colors, producing a lustrous effect. All whites, grays, and pastels must be eliminated.

Iridescence is that special effect found in mother-of-pearl, opals, and the wings of some butterflies. Iridescence is produced when a large area that is predominantly gray in tone contrasts with soft, refined, subtle tints. The background need not be completely gray but must be a hue near to it, such as grayish blue, rose, orchid, lavender, sage green, or tan. These same grayed hues may also be included in the design. Plant materials should be of clear tints, about halfway between the pure hue and white, and have no gray in their makeup.

A luminous object is bright, appearing to be lighted from within. When the sun shines through onto a small grove of trees on a gloomy, dull day, the area which is sunlit will appear luminous, in sharp contrast to the darker tones of the trees that remain under clouds. In design, this illusion of luminosity is achieved by surrounding the chosen hue with a dark value or shade of itself, or a dark hue of its opposite or complement.

Every successful arrangement depends in large part upon the colors it incorporates and the ways they relate to one another. It is helpful to have some understanding of these ever-fascinating color harmonies and effects. Though color as such is not generally stressed in flower show work, it is sometimes the focus of arrangers' guilds, judges' councils, and other study groups, or featured in the schedule of an advanced flower show. Experienced arrangers may develop an even fuller understanding of the myriad effects of color through strict color classes. Once the groundwork of this chapter is fully absorbed, however, the beginner should be ready to progress by encountering color in a more relaxed way, experientially, in each design as he or she creates it.

6 Our Roots: Early 20th-Century American Designs

Flower arranging is an outlet for our creativity, one that enriches lives and beautifies the world around us. While it is generally agreed that such a thing is good for us—actually healthy, in fact, providing as it does a welcome respite from more stressful activities—and though we resolve to engage in our preferred creative outlet regularly, today's busy lifestyle often interferes. If a design study group exists, or can be organized, it will be a great help; specific practice assignments and study sessions will keep the beginning designer focused and on target. Advanced arrangers also find such groups stimulating.

Just as one must learn to walk before learning to run, so must the aspiring flower arranger master basic Traditional design styles before advancing to Creative work. Studying pictures of successful arrangements or even watching a floral designer at work will not make one a skilled flower arranger, any more than admiring a watercolor or observing an artist apply pigment to canvas will make one a painter. This is not to say there is nothing to be gained by observing other people's successful work, but there is simply no shortcut to attaining the actual skills required by the artistic endeavor. In each instance, the student must study basic information, learn techniques, and gain skill by practice—and more practice—however faltering initial attempts may be.

For the student of floral design, an almost second-nature knowledge of the elements and principles of design, discussed in chapter four, is the first goal. Physical technique and creative skill begin with the study of a certain design style—and this chapter will provide the basics for a focus on Traditional design—but will develop only with practice.

Throughout this learning process, then, keep in mind that the elements and principles of design will always apply. As one learns to arrange plant material in the basic Traditional Line, Line-mass, and Mass design styles, even trying to recall, much less to incorporate, these tenets may seem an overwhelming task. With practice, it becomes increasingly easy—their proper use becomes habitual, accomplished almost without conscious effort. Happily, a momentary lapse on the novice's part is practically self-correcting. When a design is disturbing, and the reason is not readily apparent, a mental review of the principles and their application will usually reveal the one that has been forgotten, and the problem is soon remedied. It is sometimes helpful to walk away for a few minutes and return to look at the design from a fresh point of view.

These three Early 20th-Century American design styles are the perfect first study and a natural place to begin development of skill and technique. They are basic designs and have never lost their popularity, suitable as they are for almost any occasion and in homes of almost any style. Set rules and patterns provide a clear framework for the beginner, making it quite easy to become skilled in their creation. Once these design styles have been mastered, it is relatively simple to move on to more creative work.

That progression will be even easier nowadays, for the basic Traditional design styles of Line, Line-mass, and Mass are interpreted more creatively today than in the past. Line length especially is often longer than the strictly traditional recommendation for one-and-one-half times the height or diameter of the container. Plant material may have a slightly creative reworking; for example, a few iris leaves may be looped near the focal area. One may find, too, more striking combinations of color and texture, and lines may be more vigorous and forceful than they were in Traditional designs of the past.

Other characteristics, however, remain unchanged. All three basic Traditional design styles are planned around a set pattern and are based on the geometric forms of the cylinder, cone, cube, and sphere, or manipulations of these forms. Modifications include, for example, the extraction of the crescent from the sphere and the triangle from the cube. They are meant to be placed in a specific location or to interpret a specific theme. All proper Traditional designs will still have a certain naturalistic effect, even to representing a segment of nature. All Line, Line-mass, and Mass designs continue to hold the following traits in common:

- A single point of emergence (all lines arise from a common point).
- A single, well-defined focal area at the point of emergence.
- A single opening in the container.
- A simple container (usually in an earth color, such as black, brown, gray, or green).
- Plant material over the rim of the container (unifies the two components).
- Plant material used in uneven numbers.
- Plant material grouped by color and kind.
- Radial placement of the plant material (mimics natural growth habit).
- Longest or tallest lines one-and-one-half to two times the height or diameter of the container.
- No crossing lines.
- No two lines the same height or length.
- No two blooms placed at the same height.
- Components with greatest visual weight placed low in the design (largest forms, strongest colors, thickest lines).
- Components with the least visual weight placed at or near the top or periphery of the design (smallest forms, lightest colors, thinnest lines).
- Depth and rhythm achieved through gradation of size, color, texture, and overlapping forms.
- Transitional material used to fill spaces within the design.

- Realistic figurines used as accessories or features.
- A base or bases, often used under the design.
- Mechanics completely hidden.

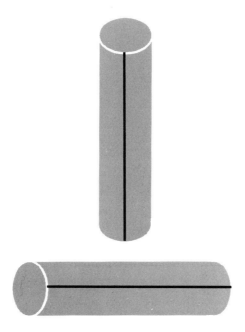

Vertical and horizontal line directions are derived from the cylinder. In combination, they produce the inverted-T pattern so popular with florists.

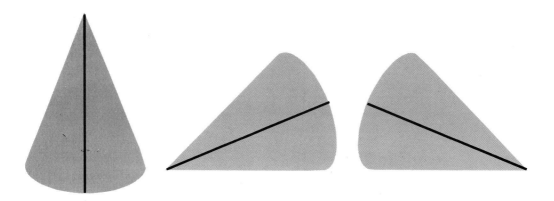

The cone provides the vertical and an infinite number of oblique line directions, including the two shown here.

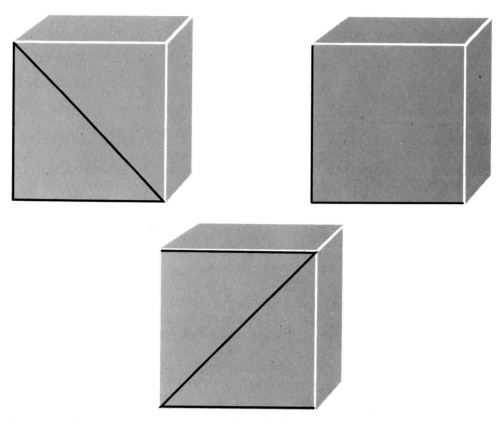

Extractions from the cube include the triangle, right angle, and zig-zag forms and lines.

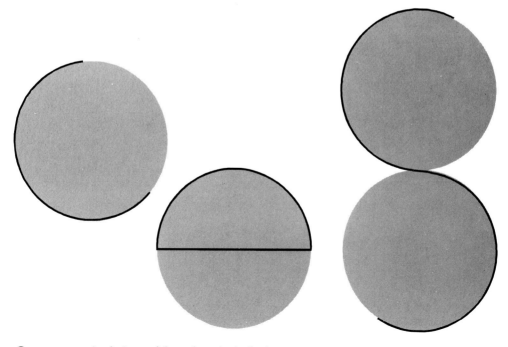

Common manipulations of the sphere include the crescent, the fan, and the Hogarth curve.

Now let us turn to the specifics of each Traditional Early 20th-Century American design style.

LINE

Line designs directly reflect the strong influence of Oriental design on flower arranging in the West. They are clean-cut designs, composed primarily, as their name implies, of line material. A minimum of flowers and foliage establishes the focal area and creates minimal depth. The open form emphasizes the beauty of plant material, the elegance of line, the silhouette of blooms and foliage, and the resulting spaces around and between them.

A single, strong line, such as a pine branch, a large bare branch, or a piece of decorative wood, will create a well-defined Line design which holds the viewer's attention. Often the addition of a few blooms and a little foliage is all that is required to achieve a dramatic design. Very light, thin material, such as iris foliage, will need to be repeated in order to strengthen the line. Several weaker lines may replace one bold line, but are inevitably less dynamic.

LINE-MASS

Line-mass designs result from the combination of Oriental Line designs and the Mass designs of Europe. They are closely related to Line designs, and it is sometimes difficult to differentiate between the two. In Line-mass designs, the line remains important, but there is more massing of plant material, creating a greater depth—the third dimension that is practically nonexistent in Line designs. Plant material is placed to form an orderly outline and massed to create a focal area, with gradual change from line at the top and outer periphery to mass at the central axis. Line-mass designs also have an open form and have either asymmetrical or symmetrical balance.

LINEAR PATTERNS

The following design forms may be either Line or Line-mass, depending upon the amount of plant material used.

Vertical

Vertical designs are very narrow, extending little beyond the rim of the container. The dominant thrust of the plant material must be vertical, with few lines leading in other directions. Line material is usually naturally tall and very straight, such as cattail, delphinium, gladiolus, iris foliage, phormium, or ting-ting. The focal area is at the lip of the container. A vertical design is more easily attained in a tall container than in a flat one. Such designs create feelings of aspiration, inspiration, and dignity.

On the left, decorative wood serves as a container in a Traditional Line-mass design. The line created by the branch of Japanese maple sweeps to the left, balancing the greater visual weight on the lower right of the design. True to Traditional style, orange Asiatic lilies and hosta foliage are arranged in their natural growth pattern. In the arrangement on the right, red carnations and a bit of foliage combine with line material for a Traditional Line design in a vertical pattern. The line material extends down into the glass container, echoing the lines above; many stems continue all the way to the bottom of the container— essential for overall visual balance.

Crescent

A crescent design should represent approximately one-half to two-thirds of a circle. It should appear as though the main structural line would meet if the two tips of the design were extended in the direction of their curve, forming a complete circle. The center of the crescent should not be filled in to any great height, as this would spoil the "new moon" effect. Balance may be either symmetrical or asymmetrical. If the tips of the crescent line are equal in height, balance is symmetrical, and the focal area should be in the center of the design. If asymmetrical balance is desired, place the tip of one end of the line higher than the tip on the opposite side. The lower curve of the line should be approximately one-half to one-fourth the length of the taller sweep of the curve. The focal area will be at the axis, where the two lines meet at their base, so the focal area will be slightly off-center. The asymmetrically balanced crescent is more appealing than the symmetrically balanced one and is also easier to achieve. Crescent designs are perennially popular as the viewer is involved in mentally completing the broken circle.

Horizontal

A horizontal design is restful and quiet. The designer has the choice of using a flat container, keeping the design very low, or a footed container, allowing the ends to curve slightly downward or upward. It is an effective design either way. Traditional horizontal designs have symmetrical or asymmetrical balance.

Hogarth

The English artist William Hogarth made frequent use of the S-curve, or what he called "the line of beauty." This design may be upright or horizontal. The two sweeps of the S are usually gracefully elongated, rather than short and sharply curved. They should meet at the needleholder, giving the impression that the line material is a single, uninterrupted entity, even if it is made up of two or more components. If balance is to be achieved, the tip of each line should curve back to the imaginary axis. The lower curve will extend slightly forward, toward the viewer, while the upper curve should lean slightly backward. The focal area should be at the center of the design, where all curves meet.

Asymmetrical triangle

The asymmetrical triangle is the most popular of the Traditional Line or Line-mass designs, perhaps because minimal amounts of plant material and effort are required to produce a design that is satisfying. In winter or late spring, three bare branches, three or more flowers, and a few large leaves will suffice. The design may be either a right- or a left-handed triangle, meaning the tallest line will be either right or left of the axis. If one were to look down upon this type of design and connect the tips of the three main thrusts of plant material with imaginary lines, these straight lines would form a triangle. The triangle will also be visible from the front and sides, but by looking down on the design it is easier to determine if adequate depth has been achieved. The design is particularly pleasing, as are all asymmetrically balanced designs.

Oblique

The main line of an oblique design is on an incline, slanting somewhere between the perpendicular and the horizontal. An oblique design depends upon dynamic balance—the placement of visually heavier material near the axis, on one side of the design, to balance the longer, visually lighter line on the opposite side. A flat or short-footed container is appropriate. The tilt of an oblique design together with the dynamic balance makes it exciting to view.

Zig-zag

The main line of a zig-zag design contains two or more sharp angles, reminiscent of lightning. A small amount of plant material is used to emphasize the focal area, where the line originates, and may extend along the line for a bit, leading the eye toward the sharp angles. This too is a restless, exciting design.

MASS

Mass designs are usually triangular, oval, circular, or fan-shaped. They are also derived from geometric forms: the triangle from the cube and oval, circular, and fan-shaped designs from the sphere. More plant material is required than in either Line or Line-mass designs. While the entire form is well filled, or closed form, the plant material is not crowded, as it was in the early European Mass designs upon which American forms are based.

There is a gradual change from strong colors and large sizes at the focal area to lighter colors and smaller sizes at the top and outer edges. These designs are almost always symmetrically balanced and quite stately or formal in mood.

A black metal compote holds a Traditional Mass design. Equal visual weight on each side of the central axis creates symmetrical balance. The various flowers and foliage have been arranged in a loose, airy manner, their colors and forms interspersed throughout the design and gradually clustered at the focal area.

The following chapter will guide the beginning designer in the step-by-step construction of four Early 20th-Century American designs. The advanced designer may wish to skip on to the Creative designs described in chapter eight.

A cherub container holds a stately Traditional Mass design aloft. The many green buds and white blooms of lilac are combined with white iris, white stock, and leucothoe. The yellow background complements the dark gold of the container, and the yellow beards of the iris continue the color coordination. In chapter nine, the same design appears in a table setting.

Flowers and fruit effectively arranged in a more stylized Traditional Mass design using the same graceful cherub container. Design by Martha Allen, Snellville, Georgia.

7 A Step-by-Step Guide to Traditional Designs

And now, before dashing off into more Creative work, we shall begin our "walk" through a handful of hands-on Traditional designs and their step-by-step arrangement. As we have said, because each follows a set pattern, any Traditional design is an ideal starting point for one's first attempt at floral design. The four designs presented here all happen to be asymmetrically balanced as well, a further boon for the novice arranger as asymmetrical balance is much more easily achieved than symmetrical balance. By actively participating in the following acts of creation, the beginner will not only develop basic skills and techniques, but confidence as well.

DESIGN ONE

Our first project, a Line-mass design on the pattern of an asymmetrical triangle, is one of the most popular of all Traditional designs. A container, a needleholder, floral clay, and a little time are almost all that is necessary. Add a modicum of well-conditioned plant material, and a pleasing arrangement is the sure result.

The container should be approximately eight to ten inches in diameter, flat, and preferably round. A baking dish or a quiche pan would do nicely if such a container were not available.

For the plant material, select three branches that have graceful lines of a clear pattern; these will make up the major lines of the design. Crabapple or flowering plum branches are among the many likely choices. Avoid branches that are stiff and straight. In winter or early spring, the bare branches that best provide these strong lines are readily available. Later in the season, flowering branches or those with foliage are acceptable substitutes, but they may have to be trimmed slightly to reveal the branching pattern. This is something that can be learned only by doing; each specimen is different. The look of a totally bare branch can be attained year-round by using a dried branch or removing all the foliage from a fresh one.

When you have the three branches in mind, cut them so that the first is slightly more than one-and-one-half to two times the diameter of the container. "Slightly more"—perhaps one or two inches—is advised because branches will require special preparations for conditioning as described in chapter two as well as recutting before they are actually used in the design. Cut the second branch three-fourths as long as the first, and the third branch three-fourths as long as the second. Condition all three branches as described in chapter two.

Five flowers of rounded form are also needed. Varying stages of development are preferred. Remember that it is difficult to find a range of development in blooms purchased at a florist's or other commercial outlet, so look to your own or a friend's garden for rounded flowers such as roses, carnations, or chrysanthemums. All five blooms should be of the same flower type, same color, and of a size similar to or slightly larger than large carnations. Choose two that are just beginning to open, two that are half open, and one fully developed bloom. Stem lengths will be settled as the design progresses, but elements to consider as you choose the five flowers are color, form, texture, and size. The color harmony should be pleasing; look for contrasts of form and texture, and be sure all materials are in scale. Remove all foliage and condition the plant material well, according to directions for its type.

Rounding out the list of required plant material will be seven short branches of foliage of varying stem lengths to be used as transitional material. Choose one—but not the longest—for its particularly large leaf. These branches too will be recut before placement in the design, but start with a selection in which the longest is approximately half the length of the longest of the three major line branches. As you choose the foliage, keep in mind the color, size, and texture of the flowers you have already selected. If the flowers are smooth in texture, as roses are, choose textured foliage—such as salal or viburnum—to provide the needed contrast. If the flowers are roughly textured, select smooth foliage; for example, pair carnations with shiny camellia or rhododendron leaves. Condition branches well.

Using floral clay, affix the needleholder to the center of the container using the press-and-twist method described in chapter two. Both the container and the needleholder must be dry for the floral clay to adhere. Pour a small amount of water in the container, enough to half cover the needleholder. The plant material suggested for this design must be kept in water at all times in order to remain fresh.

Now you are ready. Take clippers in hand and a very deep breath. Remember from time to time to compare your design's progress to the sequential illustrations in this chapter. And begin with enthusiasm!

First, recut the end of the longest branch on a slant, taking off the portion that was split during conditioning so that the remaining length is from one-and-one-half to two times the diameter of the container. This is line number one.

Insert this line vertically onto the needleholder, slightly to the back and a little left of the needleholder's center. If the branch is difficult to attach, slit it crossways on the stem end and try again. Adjust the branch so that the tip is slightly off vertical, leaning left and back. If the branch curves, bring the tip back over the axis for balance.

Recut line number two so that it is two-thirds to three-fourths the length of line number one. Place this branch toward the left front of the needleholder. Insert it vertically, then position the tip of the line at an angle toward your left shoulder, approximately halfway between the vertical and the horizontal. By placing each line vertically onto the needleholder and then adjusting it for final direction, a firmer attachment is achieved.

Recut line number three so that the remaining length is two-thirds to three-fourths the length of line number two. Insert this line vertically, then position it horizontally and to the right, pointing slightly toward you.

Check the design for balance and stability. Each piece of plant material must be perfectly stable before the next is added, or the pieces will fall over at later stages. When one looks down on the design at this point, the tips of the three main lines should form a spreading asymmetrical triangle.

Next comes the placement of some foliage, used transitionally in the design. Reserve the branch with the largest leaf for use in defining the focal area in a later step. Recut the longest foliage branch so that it is approximately one-third the length of line number one. Place it next to and a little toward the front of line number one. Recut the next-longest foliage branch so that it is approximately two-thirds the length of the foliage branch just positioned. Place it close to line number two, a little toward the front and center. Recut and place the third-longest branch of foliage close by and to the left of line number three. Recut and place the fourth and fifth branches toward the front of the needleholder—one left of center and the other right of center. The center of the needleholder must be left open for the insertion of the flowers and the last foliage at the focal area.

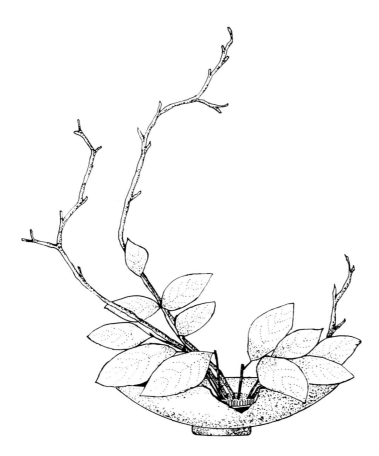

Design One: A cutaway of the container showing the needleholder and the placement of line material and initial foliage before flowers are added.

Now for the placement of the flowers. First, let's develop some depth in the back of the design. Choose the tallest of the two smallest, just-opening blooms—preferably a little shorter than the first piece of foliage—and place it on the needleholder by and slightly behind line number one. Next, choose the shorter of the two half-open blooms and place it toward the middle of the needleholder, closely following the direction of line number two. It should be slightly lower and forward of the first bloom and appear just inside the branching of line number two.

Cut the stem of the remaining just-opening flower so that it is one-third the length of line number three, but shorter than the foliage branches surrounding it. Place this flower inside the branching of line number three toward the middle of the needleholder. The remaining half-opened bloom, slightly taller than the one already positioned, is placed on the back center of the needleholder; lean it a little toward the back of the design to help create depth.

Design One: A cutaway showing the placement and positioning of the first four flowers.

The last flower—the largest, fully open bloom—is placed in the center of the design to help form the focal area. It should tip ever so slightly toward the front and must be either a little taller or little shorter than the third bloom we placed, the just-opening one that accompanies line number three.

Now the design is ready for the finishing touches. Trim the large leaf and a bit of branch from the reserved foliage. Place it so that the leaf issues from beneath the last-positioned, full-blown flower—thereby strengthening and completing the focal area—and continues toward the front of the design. It should extend out over the rim of the container but not touch the table. Use the last short piece of foliage—perhaps trimmed to include only one or two large leaves—to refine the back of the design and create additional depth. Place it low in the container on a horizontal plane. Very little of this foliage will actually be seen from the front of the design, but it affects visual balance and finishes off the back nicely. Unless the design is free-standing, it is not necessary to have as much depth in the back as in the front, but one must never leave the back of a design in an obviously unfinished state.

Now, look at your design to see if any adjustments are needed. It should look very much like the finished design pictured. Place your arrangement in its intended spot, fill the container with water, and enjoy!

Design One: The finished arrangement.

DESIGN TWO

Our second exercise—a Line-mass design on an asymmetrically balanced oblique line pattern—is a very simple one of fruit and foliage, suitable for a casual breakfast or luncheon table. For it, you will need two apples (three if using water picks), three small bananas, one or two bunches of grapes (depending on size), five branches of ivy, a flat container, and either a cupholder or water picks.

All fruit should be firm, fresh, well formed, and slightly underripe. Each type of fruit must be in scale with the other types. Select apples that vary in size; gradation here will add interest. Choose clusters of grapes that are classically full near the stem end and gradually tapering toward the tip. The bananas should be attached to one another and slightly curved.

Consider color in making your selections. For a subtle color harmony, choose yellow-green apples and green grapes to blend with the yellow-green of the bananas and the green of the ivy foliage. A harmony using dark red apples and deep red-violet grapes would be an attractive alternate combination—the choice is yours.

Choose a flat container, either round or square, in a size that is in scale with the fruit and of a color that will complement the intended color harmony, whether contrasting or monochromatic.

Select five well-formed stems of ivy; these too should be fuller at the cut stem end, gradually tapering in size toward the tip, and well covered with foliage all along their lengths. If the ivy is very thin, with small foliage, two branches of varying lengths may be used together to make up "one" branch of the proper fullness. Cut the longest branch so that it is the same length as the diameter of the container. Wash the ivy in tepid water, recut stem ends, and condition for several hours or overnight.

The cupholder will only need to accommodate the five stems of ivy, so choose one that is very small. Place it in the back center of the container. Water picks would serve as an alternate method of providing the necessary moisture to the ivy.

Place the bunch of bananas on its side, positioning it so that the stem end is near the center of the container, with the bananas curving off toward the right and ending slightly forward. Always place fruit with the stem toward the center of the design, mimicking its natural growth habit.

Place the largest apple left of center and a little toward the front half of the container, stem pointing inward. Recut the longest branch of ivy and place it in the cupholder or a water pick; create with it an oblique line leading off toward the left of the design. Recut a second ivy branch to approximately three-fourths the length of the first. Place it in the available source of moisture, and extend it to create a horizontal line toward the right front of the design. Follow the curve of the bananas, then extend the tip to the right.

Place the grapes (one bunch may be sufficient if it is a large one) with the tip curving off-center and to the right. If a cupholder is used, place the second apple directly atop it, close to the cluster of grapes. If water picks are used, a third apple may be necessary to raise the level of the second so that it too will appear close by the cluster of grapes.

Recut a third ivy branch approximately two-thirds the length of the first and place it close to and leading in the same direction as branch number one to strengthen this line. Recut the fourth ivy branch so that it is two-thirds the length of the one just placed. Insert this ivy branch between the two featured apples and into the source of moisture, angling the tip toward the left front. Add another short stem of ivy in the back between the apple and the bananas, extending the tip up and toward the back. Compare your arrangement to the completed design pictured and make any necessary adjustments.

A similar design may be made with the addition of a few simple flowers—perhaps yellow or white daisies—placed along the lines created by the ivy, with three or four blooms clustered at the focal area.

Design Two: The placement of the cupholder, bananas, one of the apples, and the first two branches of ivy.

Design Two: The finished arrangement.

DESIGN THREE

The next arrangement is a Line design on a triangular pattern, asym-metrically balanced and very much in the spare Oriental manner. It is a very simple design, requiring—besides a container and needleholder—only three iris blooms and some iris foliage. Choose iris that are naturally curved as such stems are more easily managed later in the creation of this design. Condition the iris for several hours. Remove the foliage, reserving six leaves of varying heights. Condi-tion them as well.

Choose a footed container for this design, though a flat one will do. Adhere a small needleholder to the center of the container; the needleholder should be small enough—about one-and-one-half inches in diameter—to be almost entirely filled when all plant material has been inserted into it. Partially fill the container with water.

Once again, the dimensions of the container are crucial when determining the length of plant material. If you are using a footed container, add together its diameter and height. If the container has no foot, consider the diameter alone. Cut the stem of the smallest bloom so that it is one-and-one-half to two times the "measurement" of the container. This will be the design's tallest line. Place this iris vertically in the center of the needleholder.

The second stem should be cut to approximately two-thirds the length of the first stem. Place it close behind and to the left of the first, initially on the vertical. Gently massage a curve into the stem so that it closely follows the first stem for at least three inches before curving off to the left back of the container. This adjust-ment is accomplished with a minimum of pressure if a naturally curved stem has been selected. The key word here is "gently"—too much pressure all at once and the stem will snap, and the whole of selection, conditioning, cutting, and placement begins once more. Slow and steady is the much better way!

The remaining stem should be cut to approximately two-thirds the length of the second stem. Place this stem close to the first as well, but in front of it and a little to the right. It too should follow the line of the first stem for at least three inches before curving off, this time to the right front. Position the stem so that the bloom is toward your right shoulder. The bloom should tilt slightly up toward bloom number one; once again, if the stem does not naturally curve, it will require some careful manipulation. Work the stem gently until the desired curve is obtained.

Next is the placement of the additional iris foliage. Place one leaf as close to the front of the first iris stem as possible. The leaf should be only an inch or two taller than the stem and curve to the left at the tip just in front of the bloom. Add a second leaf directly behind this first stem to strengthen the line. This leaf should curve to the right behind the bloom. When placing foliage, remember that no two leaves should be exactly the same height, and they should always follow the line created by the bloom stem for most of its length.

A third leaf is placed in front of the second iris stem, and a fourth leaf is placed as close behind the bloom of the second iris stem as possible. These leaves should be placed in the same positions as those in front of and behind the first bloom stem. One of these leaves should be a little taller than the iris stem, the other a little shorter. All three lines, two of foliage and the one bloom stem, unite to strengthen this line of the design.

Place a fifth leaf directly in front of the third iris stem. The last of the six leaves is cut so that it is approximately halfway between the lengths of the first and second iris stems. Position it so that its tip is approximately midway between the second and third iris stems. Bend the sixth leaf in half at a sharp angle as illustrated.

Compare the design one last time to the illustration of the completed arrangement and make any necessary adjustments. If desired, add a few polished black stones at the base of the needleholder for visual balance. Do not fill the container with water until it is in its final location.

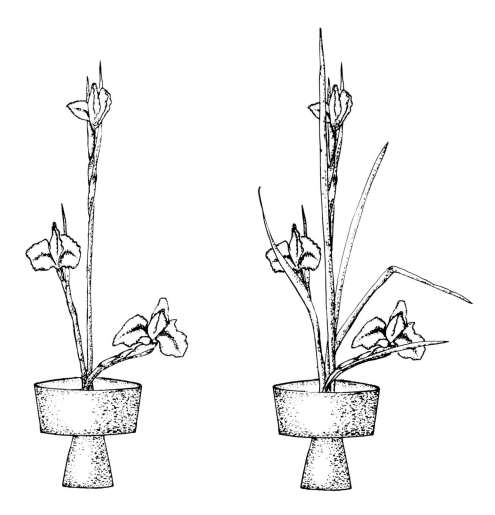

Design Three: For this design in the Oriental manner, the usual order of placement is reversed. On the left, the three iris bloom stems are placed first, before foliage. On the right, the finished arrangement.

DESIGN FOUR

Our last creation is a Line design, asymmetrically balanced, with a combination pattern of vertical and oblique. Reminiscent of the period just prior to the development of Creative designs, it will display more creativity than the three we have just worked on.

Cut seven stems of a long, slender, pliable plant material for line. Something like the blades of an ornamental grass or reed, the foliage of spuria iris or gladiolus, or even limber, unbranched stems from a shrub or tree—with all foliage removed—would do. Three roses in a variety of sizes and developmental stages and five rather small but variously sized hosta leaves will also be required. Condition all plant material properly.

Select a tall container, and place a needleholder near its top in the manner described in chapter two. Partially fill with water.

Cut four of the line stems to one-and-one-half to two times the height of the container. Recut the second line so that it is approximately three inches shorter than the first. Place these two lines in the center of the needleholder and a little to the back. These first and second lines will remain perfectly straight and vertical. Keep them as close together as possible at their shared point of emergence from the needleholder. The shorter of the two should be behind the first and may tip a little to the right near the top. Together, they will constitute the longest vertical line in the design.

The third and fourth line stems will be shaped into loops, formed in your hand and then placed in the design. Take the third line in hand, keeping its base at the right and bringing its tip down to the left. Adjust the loop just created, pulling its tip end through your thumb and fingers, until it is approximately two-thirds the height of the main vertical line (lines one and two).

Still holding this loop tightly in hand, add the fourth line stem to its left and form another loop in the same way. Adjust the size of this second loop, pulling down on the tip of the stem, so that it is approximately two-thirds the height of the first loop. Holding both loops firmly, trim off the excess at the tip ends and fasten the loops together with transparent tape. Place this pair of loops, now one unit, as close to the main vertical line as possible, on the left.

Take the remaining three stem lines in hand and adjust them to any pleasing set of differing lengths, with the longest at two-thirds the length of the main vertical line. Fan the ends slightly as illustrated. Cut off the excess at the bases and fasten them together in this position with transparent tape.

Place these stems to the right and slightly toward the front of the needleholder, reserving enough space between the vertical line and this unit to allow for the insertion of the roses and hosta leaves later in the design process. Bend this last grouping at a sharp angle about one-half inch above the rim of the container, with the ends positioned toward the table at approximately a forty-five degree angle.

Now for the placement of the flowers. Remove the leaves from all three roses. Select the smallest and cut its stem so that it is a bit shorter than the second loop. Place this rose very close to the main vertical line and directly in front of it.

Of the remaining two roses, choose the one that is closest to the first in size, but a little larger. Cut it to approximately two-thirds the length of the first, and place it in front and slightly to the right of the first rose.

The third rose should be the largest of the three in size and the most well-developed form. Cut the stem and place the rose in the front center of the needleholder, positioning it so that it appears just above the angled line material on the right of the design.

Last we shall incorporate the hosta foliage. Select the smallest hosta leaf and place it behind and to the right of the second rose. Angle it down and slightly toward the back.

Two hosta leaves will accompany the largest rose and help define the focal area. Choose one of the two mid-sized hosta leaves and place it to the right of the bloom, angled down and to the right. Take the largest hosta leaf and position it in front of the largest rose, emerging from beneath it. Angle it down and slightly to the left. The focal area is now complete.

The last two hosta leaves will be used to finish off the back of the design. Place one leaf in the back with the tip angled toward the left, allowing only the tip to be seen from the front. This placement helps create balance and depth. Place the last leaf vertically and position it down and back until the leaf lies in a horizontal plane, about one-half inch above the lip of the container. This last placement will not be seen from the front but adds to the minimal depth found in Line designs.

Place the design in its final viewing spot and fill the container with water.

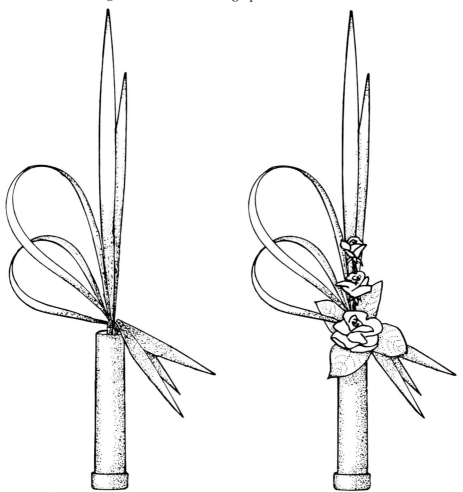

Design Four: The placement of the line material.

Design Four: The finished arrangement.

Once mastered, these four basic designs lend themselves to many themes and variations. One possibility is the simple substitution of one plant material for another when a certain form or line is all that a specific design requires. As we have learned, the round form of an allium may replace the round form of a mum, just as a line of bamboo may replace a line of pampas grass. To paraphrase Gertrude Stein: A round form is a round form is a round form. If the elements are clearly understood, the possibilities are endless.

Experiment as well with unexpected plant material, different color combinations, and both striking and subtle contrasts of form, texture, line, pattern, and size. Such variations are the main avenue of creativity in Traditional designs. Once Traditional designs have been thoroughly explored in these ways, the move into Creative work is quite simple—and the change may be so gradual that it comes as a surprise. The most difficult adjustment may result from the fact that Creative designs use much less plant material, and the true Traditionalist may have problems with this concept at first. Flower arrangers have a saying that may help ease the transition: If in doubt, leave it out!

8 Breaking Away: A Catalog of Creative Designs

By the middle of the 20th century, interest in flower arranging had reached new heights, not only in the United States but worldwide. Designing with plant material was increasingly recognized as a legitimate art form, and arrangers found themselves at once inspired by the past and freed from its restrictions. They began to study other art forms in more depth, as well as to examine and thereby reflect more closely the ever-changing world around them. Fast on the heels of the Naturalism of the 19th century and with plant material as their chosen medium, it is not surprising that flower arrangers, like the artists preceding them, continued to be greatly influenced by nature.

Abstract art fascinated many of these arrangers, who went on to incorporate abstract qualities into their floral designs. Other arrangers also felt the desire to break away from the set patterns and strict rules of Traditional designs, but found abstract art unappealing. The experimentation and ingenuity of these two groups are apparent in today's Creative designs, all of which may have some abstract qualities.

As in many other endeavors, even the very latest progressions in flower arranging are based in some part on the achievements of yesterday. Many Creative flower arrangements are clearly adaptations of floral designs from the past, yet they reflect the modern world. Several of the currently popular designs are new variations on much earlier designs. Abstract art itself is not new; the cave drawings left us by early man are nothing less than abstracted forms—symbolically rather than intentionally abstract perhaps, but abstractions nonetheless.

As to form, Assemblages, Collages, and Constructions—all popular styles in Creative work—were directly inspired by earlier art forms. The chief difference is that flower arrangers include plant material in their adaptations and must possibly modify their work with the special requirements of the flower show in mind.

This is not to say that entirely new types of designs will not emerge; it is inevitable that they should in an era which encourages and supports the development of creativity. Inventiveness, originality, and ingenuity all play a role in the creative process, together with a sense of discovery and play. Today's designers

This simple arrangement reflects the eclecticism of Creative designs. The container, monkey puzzle vine, and corkscrew willow combine to create a rhythmic, repetitive flow of line, accented by chrysanthemums and hosta leaves.

are free to ply their skills, exploring endless possibilities, knowing that nothing should be rejected simply because it is new or has not been seen before. The world will continue to change, and flower arranging must change, creatively, along with it.

Creativity allows the designer this freedom: to produce a design that is spontaneous, imaginative, reflective of the world, and expressive of the artist's innermost feelings. What we have seen and done; where we have been; how we reacted and what we later recall—all affect the art we create as we try to make the intangible tangible. A Creative design is a visible extension of an artist's mood and thought, a way for the artist to convey these unique feelings to an audience. Moreover, the product of the artist's personal inspiration will evoke a different response in each viewer, who sees the artwork through his or her own personal sensibility.

Each of us and the art forms we create are greatly influenced not only by our personal experience, but by the larger events of the period in which we live. In today's fast-paced world, time seems limited and therefore more precious; as artists, we are more likely to produce one large, dramatic design than several small arrangements.

The "inventive" aspect of creativity forces the artist to view the familiar in a new way. For the designer, the first step toward creativity may be as simple as searching for something that will do as a container; using familiar plant material in a new way; arranging common components to create a new form; or combining colors and textures not usually used together. Creative designs are eclectic in spirit, borrowing from different styles and periods and combining these features into a thoroughly original, well-integrated concept or form.

Creative designs have few rules and no set patterns. Designs are usually bold in color, form, and size, yet show great restraint in the amount of plant material and number of components used. They may have more than one point of emergence, more than one focal area and some abstraction. If a container is used in the design—and it need not be—it is almost always non-Traditional, with several openings. It is not necessary to use all the openings, nor is it required that the container be subordinate to plant material and other components. A brightly colored, shiny container may be an asset in a Creative design. Sometimes two or more containers are used together in a creative manner.

Spatial relationships play a major role in Creative designs; they are designs of space, not merely designs within an allotted space. Space is incorporated into the design and interacts with other components. An interpenetration of space occurs, with spaces and solids becoming one. In fact, all elements in a Creative design are considered solids, either *in* or *of* space, and are equally important to the scheme. All are organized to achieve great depth in the design, and each component, solid or spatial, maintains its own character even as it relates to other components and to the design as a whole. This is known as plastic organization.

As we have noted, Creative designs, like all designs, are based on the geometric forms of the cube, cone, cylinder, and sphere, though in Creative designs these forms may be manipulated or combined into an almost unrecognizable form. A sharper eye than is necessary in Traditional work may be needed to identify the particular form upon which the design is based.

A Creative design with two points of emergence. The manzanita branch has been secured to the container using hot glue and can be removed without damage to either. Ting-ting of the same color unites the two. Caladium leaves placed in a natural growth pattern complete the design.

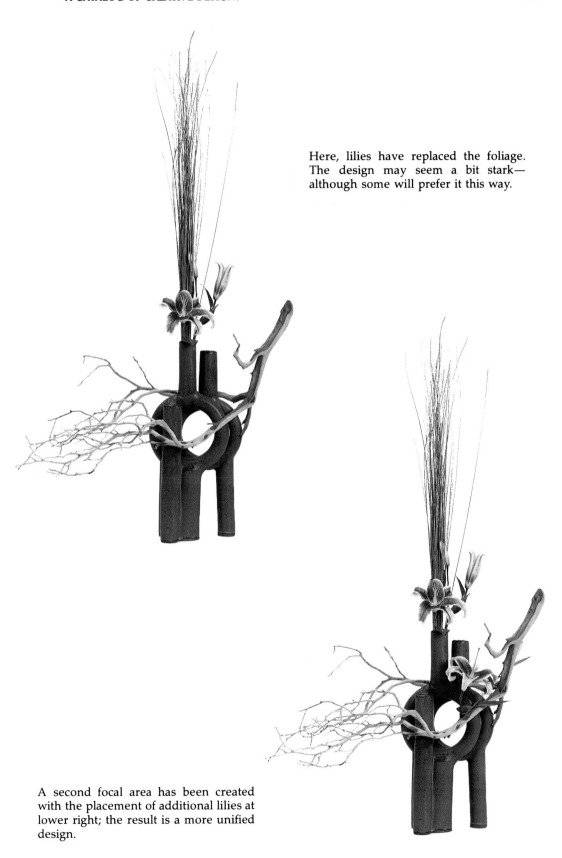

Here, lilies have replaced the foliage. The design may seem a bit stark— although some will prefer it this way.

A second focal area has been created with the placement of additional lilies at lower right; the result is a more unified design.

In this Creative design, the wisteria vine seen on page 60 has been positioned in a different direction in another container, illustrating the versatility of good line material. Stems of yellow gladiolus slash upward, penetrating the spaces formed by the vine and continuing beyond. The looped ti leaves and the oblique sweep of phormium and yellow lilies balance the enclosed spaces.

Space plays an important role in this design as well: the unique curvilinear forms of the container are repeated by the loops of monkey puzzle vine. The foliage has been abstracted by clipping, and the muted tones of the creamy apricot-pink anthuriums demonstrate that bold colors are not always a requisite in Creative work.

Banana blossoms and ti leaves carefully isolated in space allow the viewer to enjoy the simplicity of form and color in this Creative design. Tiny, immature bananas have been retained on the stems, adding unexpected color and texture. The luscious, bold, pink blooms are delicately balanced by the pink-edged foliage.

Lavender liatris follows the upward lead of black ting-ting. The black Tangle™ (a movable sculpture composed of rotating, connecting links) repeats the open spaces of the smokey black plexiglass container. Yellow lilies and gold-edged hosta foliage complete this Creative design.

The principles of design, though not set aside entirely, are applied to Creative designs in a different manner than they are to Traditional designs. Elements may be exaggerated in size. There may be no gradation between a very small and a very large element. Typical color combinations may be ignored in favor of new harmonies that would have been unthinkable in Traditional designs. In Creative design, one finds greater tension, unpredictable rhythms, and more designs which are dynamically or asymmetrically balanced.

Those who wish to arrange flowers for their own enjoyment are guided only by personal taste, what they find appealing, materials available, and the principles of design. If a design is planned for a flower show, however, the schedule may determine what is permitted or required. It sometimes stipulates an actual type of design (an alphabetical list of these design types and their descriptions will make up the bulk of this chapter) and at other times simply calls for a Creative or Abstract design, with no further specifications. In this case, as long as the arranger adheres to the principles of design and remains within the parameters of the policy of the sponsoring organization, the designer is completely free to follow his or her fancies and to create.

Flower show policies of the National Council of State Garden Clubs are spelled out in their *Handbook for Flower Shows.* National Council currently classifies all non-Traditional designs, including Abstract, under the rather broad term *Creative.* Some Creative designs will not fall into any of the specified design types; others may fit into more than one classification.

The following design types and descriptions, presented here in alphabetical order, are based primarily on the styles now recognized by National Council. All are Creative, meaning they may have some abstract qualities or—because Abstracts are included under Creative—a dominance of abstraction. If a design type must be an abstract concept it will be described as an Abstract design. Most are suitable for home or flower show, and the guidelines given here should be helpful in either case. Special considerations applicable only to flower shows are sometimes included in the description. Table designs will be discussed fully in the chapter to follow.

ABSTRACT

Abstract designs are those in which components, including the all-important element of space, are significant purely as line, form, texture, and/or color. Though the plant material and other components can usually be identified even after manipulation, they are not chosen as identifiable objects. A yellow chrysanthemum is not used because it is a yellow chrysanthemum. It is used as a round, yellow, textured form; to create interest; to give a pause point; or to stop the eye. With the elimination of the unnecessary, a new image results which is the designer's perception of a subject and its essence.

Space, depth, areas of tension, an emphasis on the interpenetration of space, and interest equated throughout the design are all characteristics common to the Abstract style. There is no gradual change in color, size, and texture between one juxtaposed element and another; transitional materials are not included as they always are in Traditional designs.

Simplicity is key in Abstract designs. The artist uses only that which is absolutely necessary to express an idea or feeling. Each component must be an essential part of the design; one should be able to look at the design and feel that nothing could be added, nothing removed. Components should be placed in such a way that not only is interest equated throughout the design, but also a tension exists between the areas of interest. This push-pull tension, with the eye of the viewer being pulled from one area to another, is important because there should be no one focal area in an Abstract design. The design must have great depth and be pleasing from all sides; the few exceptions to this requirement will be noted.

Most components of Abstract designs are bold in color and form and large in size, with an overall effect of masculinity. Though it is possible to use soft, delicate colors and small forms, it is more difficult to create an Abstract design with such elements.

There are no set patterns for or limitations to the types of material, colors, or combinations used as components of Abstract design. Components are often man-made items not generally associated with flower arranging: glass, metal, plexiglass, rope, wire. Natural items such as antlers, shells, or rocks are often included as well. Each item should be selected for its contribution to the design according to design principles; nothing should ever be included simply to shock the viewer.

Containers, if used, are almost always non-Traditional, with several openings. The container need not be subordinate to plant material. Mechanics are sometimes difficult, as the openings in this type of container will seldom accommodate a needleholder or oasis. For this reason, exotic plant material is often utilized; anthuriums, birds-of-paradise, ginger, protea, and other tropicals are extremely popular, lasting as they do for days out of water. Happily, many non-Traditional containers will require no special mechanics, as components may be arranged so that they hold one another firmly in place. When mechanics are necessary, they need not be entirely hidden if they appear to be a part of the design, are neat, and do not detract from other components or the design as a whole.

Black bamboo has been placed to extend the strong architectural lines of the container in
this simple design. Three pincushion protea vie for the attention of the viewer in typical
Abstract fashion.

Bloom spikes of bromeliad echo the color and texture of the container in this Abstract design. The foliage has been hot-glued to the container, repeating its horizontal planes. The smooth texture of the foliage contrasts well with the roughness of the other components, and the blue background is in pleasing contrast to the pink and red-violet of the plant material and container.

To abstract plant material is to divorce it from naturalism or realism. Unconventional selection and placement, or alteration by some other means, creates new line, form, shape, or texture. Some, or all, plant material in Abstract designs is placed in a non-Traditional manner: upside down, sideways, suspended in space, even moving. Plant material may be clustered to create a new form, or fastened together to create a new pattern. There should be little or no radial placement of plant material. Bending, clipping, folding, knotting, tying, or some other means of manipulation will further abstract plant material. This distortion should not be an end in itself, but a means to an end, an integral part of a well-formulated design concept. A word of caution: too much repetition of the same means of abstraction, whether through selection, placement, or manipulation, may render even the most creative concept trite.

Designers must also be aware that the qualities of the medium are somewhat restrictive, limiting the types of plant material suitable and the possible methods of abstraction. In flower shows, if the schedule permits, dried plant material may be painted to change its color or have something added to change its texture. Fresh plant material, however, may never be painted or otherwise treated to alter color or texture. The only exception is in a holiday show, where a small amount of embellishment may be added to fresh greens.

In flower show work, Abstract designs are of two types: expressive or decorative. Expressive Abstract designs have a title or theme that must be interpreted. Decorative Abstract designs have no title or theme and are non-objective, created solely for decorative effect.

ASSEMBLAGE

Art critics of another medium have credited Picasso and Braque with creating the prototypical Asemblages in the early 1900s. Their works of art, incorporating a variety of objects from everyday life, were either free-standing or mounted on a panel. By the middle of the 20th century, flower arrangers had adapted Assemblages to their own purposes and, with the addition of plant material, made them their own.

For the flower arranger, an Assemblage is an Abstract design combining diverse objects and plant material into a unified whole. It is composed of several unattached parts, or several parts fastened together to form a single unit. Using previously unrelated found objects and plant material for artistic effect, the color, form, and texture of the various elements are related anew to create a fresh identity.

Found objects may be either man-made, such as metal, plastic, rope, and wire, or natural objects, such as shells, stones, and wood. Those that are man-made need not have been previously used; manufacturing firms often discard or make available at little cost items which can be quite useful to the flower arranger. The observant flower arranger will select and display such objects in a manner which emphasizes their unique qualities of form, contour, color, and texture.

Components are juxtaposed—placed side by side or overlapping one another—with or without a connective, to create a unified design. The overall concept must be Abstract, but all elements need not be abstracted.

There are four types of Assemblages in flower show work. The Type I Assemblage is composed, as are all Assemblages, of plant material and unrelated objects placed together to create a design in relation to a defined frame of reference. In a home, this frame of reference may be the expanse of wall behind a piece of furniture; in a flower show, it may be a space provided on a table or by a background or niche. If a background or niche is used, it must be an integral part of the overall design, not simply a defining of space allotted. It is not enough to unify the background or niche and the design itself merely through color; more is required to integrate the two. For instance, one or more components may be attached to the background or niche, appearing to be a continuation of the design, an active part of the whole.

A Type II Assemblage is a free-standing, three-dimensional form staged on a pedestal, open column, or other upright structure. It is created in relation to the size of the structure upon which it is displayed. Objects used should be—or appear to be—permanently attached to one another. They may extend beyond the top of the structure but must be well balanced and stable. A pedestal or open column is an effective way to display an arrangement in a home as well as in a flower show.

In a Type III Assemblage, three-dimensional objects and plant material are fastened to a panel. Such an Assemblage has three dimensions, all of which may be controlled by the schedule, and differs from the two-dimensional Collage, which has only height and width but no depth. The smaller the height and width of the panel, the less depth is required to attain a correct, pleasing proportion. Conversely, with greater height and width, a greater depth may be necessary. Proportionate depth, however, will seldom exceed a few inches as a Type III Assemblage is designed to be hung on a wall and would appear awkward and ungainly if too deep. Weathered boards, plexiglass, or other rigid materials may be used as the panel. Artist's canvas boards are another excellent choice as they are sufficiently rigid, lighter in weight than plywood or other wood products, and easily obtained and transported. Their surface is ready to use as is; it may also be painted or covered with fabric or some other type of material. Dried plant material is often used in Type III Assemblages, but with a little foresight, fresh plant material may also be included. Space can be set aside on the panel for the insertion of water picks to provide the needed water supply.

A Type IV Assemblage is some combination of two or more of the other types, allowing great creativity. For example, the designer might stage a free-standing Assemblage on a pedestal (Type II) against or with an Assemblage on a panel (Type III) and both might be staged within a frame, niche, or against a background (Type I). Coordination within such a complicated grouping is an important factor and may be accomplished through repetition of color, texture, type of plant material, or other components.

A Type III Assemblage, with overlapping forms of plexiglass, felt-covered wood scraps, and decorative wood glued in place on a flat panel. The required plant material, a single stem of gladiolus, repeats the color pink and provides another form. The wood has been strategically positioned to conceal a water pick.

BOTANICAL

In a Botanical design, plant material, whether fresh or dried, is chosen for its high horticultural quality and must dominate the arrangement by virtue of its color, form, placement, and/or texture. Other components, either natural or man-made, are often used as line material to emphasize and enhance the featured plant material and direct the attention of the viewer to it.

Occasionally, the schedule requires that fresh plant material be featured instead of dry. In any case, though it need not have been grown by the exhibitor, the plant material must have been grown in a non-professional home setting, indoors or out, garden or greenhouse. No plant material from a florist or professional grower may be used in a Botanical design in flower shows.

Though the plant material must be of high horticultural quality, it need not be of horticulture specimen quality. In horticulture classes, uniformity is extremely important; all specimens in a multiple-specimen class will be at their peak of perfection as well as at the same degree of development. In a Botanical design, this is not required or even particularly desirable. The designer is free to choose curved branches over straight, or to use blooms of varying sizes and at several stages of development, from buds to partially and fully open inflorescences.

Plant material used in Botanical designs should not be abstracted by any means other than by placement, or altered in any manner that would be unacceptable in a horticulture class. For instance, the tip of a gladiolus may be snapped out in other sorts of designs, but as this is not permitted in horticulture classes, neither is it permissible in a Botanical design. Though florists sometimes use plants with the bulbs or roots still attached—and washed clean—in what they call botanical designs, National Council does not allow the use of living, rooted plants in any design.

A single spray of lilies properly dominates this Botanical design. The line material of monkey puzzle vine is not only a subtle, seamless match of the container's color, but appears to be a continuation of the decorative lines adorning it.

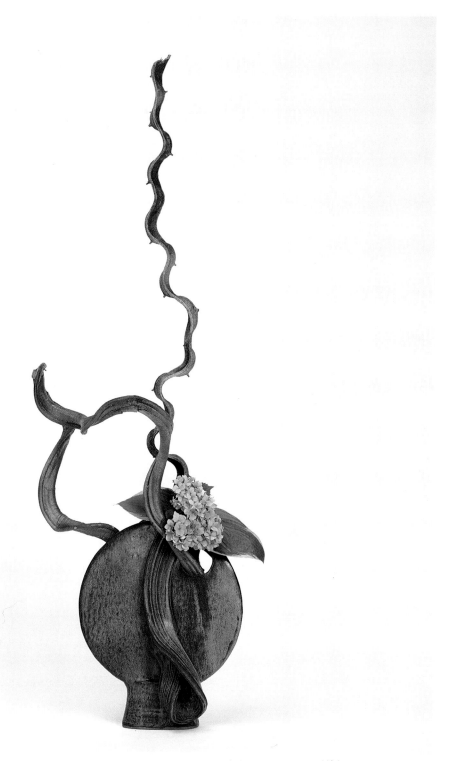

Here, a new line of vine, perfectly proportioned for a container of this size, has been introduced vertically, and the line material is now dominant. In addition, the blue hydrangea and hosta foliage lack the presence of the lilies. The new design is Creative, certainly, but it is no longer a Botanical.

COLLAGE

Collage, a term derived from the French word for paste or glue, refers to the technique of gluing seemingly unrelated, two-dimensional objects onto a flat panel. As *papiers collés*, literally "pasted papers," collage was considered a recreational craft in the 19th century; by 1913, Picasso and Braque were incorporating ordinary objects into their Cubist paintings to represent planes and add textures. Folded paper, glass, newspaper clippings, sand, strips of paper, tickets, wire, and wood were some of the flat, or nearly so, items they employed.

Pressing flowers had been perennially popular, and toward the middle of the 20th century, flower arrangers took the natural step of adapting collages for use with the medium of plant material. The Collage in floral design is a two-dimensional, Abstract design of unrelated found objects—naturally occurring and man-made—and plant material, arranged in juxtaposition, and pasted, glued, or otherwise attached to a flat panel. Paint is often included as a unifying element.

Collages have height and width but very minimal depth. In such a scheme, color and texture become important considerations. As in a painting, depth is implied rather than actual and is often obtained through overlapping forms. Like the final design as a whole, all components must be two-dimensional, even the required plant material: usually dried or pressed flowers, ferns, foliage, or grasses.

Collages are evocative conversation pieces for the home, office, or public space and are often framed under glass for protection and preservation. Besides being exhibited alone, Collages are frequently included in flower shows by incorporating them into the background of another design or as an art object with a coordinated flower arrangement.

"Le Courrier" (1913), a collage in charcoal gouache and printed paper by French artist Georges Braque (1882–1963). Philadelphia Museum of Art: A. E. Gallatin Collection.

Artist's canvas board serves as the panel for this two-dimensional Collage of acrylic paint, corrugated cardboard, colored paper, and dried, clipped palm leaves. The board is painted in an abstract pattern of very bright colors, and cardboard and paper have been torn for a rough-edged effect. The half-leaf, whose outline is echoed in the light green paper it over-laps, creates tension. All components are glued to the panel in a painterly, overlapping fashion. Turn the page to any position: you will see that there is no right or wrong perspective—a good test of abstraction in this type of design.

Floral works of art can be coordinated for dramatic effect. This Creative arrangement, planned with the Collage in mind, repeats the colors and textures of the brown palm leaves and cardboard with the decorative, textured portion of the container. The iris provides contrast of both texture and color. The exaggerated height of the design leads the eye into the Collage.

CONSTRUCTION

A Construction is a design which has above all a strong architectural quality. Though it must seem to be a single unit, it is actually a creation of a minimum number of types of materials, most often only one or two, whose parts are attached or appear to be so.

Man-made materials, such as lumber or plexiglass, or strong-lined plant material—such as bamboo, equisetum, mullein, palm spathes, or tree branches—make up a typical Construction. Creative flower arrangers will think of many other elements which would do as well. Additional plant material is always required to enhance the Construction, regardless of the type of material—man-made or natural—from which the form itself is constructed.

A Construction requires a limited number of types of materials; an Assemblage differs as it must be Abstract, requires the use of unrelated components, and may use a larger number of components. Constructions are often pictured in the Ikebana books of various schools, but are listed as Abstract or Free-style designs.

Tree branches have been joined together and painted a subdued brown to create this versatile Construction. Here, it is enhanced by pink anthuriums, eucalyptus foliage, and the contrast of rough-textured juniper. The Construction would be equally interesting on its side or elevated by a rod, and might easily serve as staging for a table design.

CREATIVE LINE

Unlike a Traditional Line design, the boldly dramatic, open-form Creative Line design has no set pattern and may have more than one focal area, some abstraction, and possibly more than one point of emergence. The emphasis is on line, contrast of form, and texture. Plant material is kept to a minimum, with the beauty of individual blooms and foliage further emphasized by their skillful placement. Either plant material or man-made or found objects may be used as line material. Too much plant material tends to destroy created spaces and detract from the line; if too many components are used, the resulting design would be a Creative Line-mass, not a Creative Line design.

Creative Line designs are further categorized by the direction of the line. A Creative Horizontal Line design is usually asymmetrical and placed in a frame of reference with more width then height. Its dominant thrust is horizontal. Though it need not be absolutely horizontal, the eye of the viewer should be engaged to move in a single horizontal pass over the design.

With the exception of line direction and a frame of reference with more height than width to strengthen it, a Creative Vertical Line design has all the qualities of the Creative Horizontal Line, and the same precautions must be taken to preserve its vertical thrust and guide the eye toward the vertical. For a Creative Oblique Line design, with its movement of line approximately halfway between the vertical and horizontal, extra care must be taken to balance the components along the oblique line. A Creative Zig-zag Line design is another possible direction a Creative Line design might take, or the line may be a combination of these varying line directions. Unless the schedule specifies the line direction, the choice is up to the arranger, and the only criteria is that the design be predominantly line.

Above, a dynamically balanced Creative Horizontal Line design, combining pink carnations, variegated ti leaves, and decorative wood. The wood and looped ti leaves left of the axis combine to balance the long line of wood and carnations on the right.

Below, a Creative Oblique Line design with fasciated asparagus placed to create dynamic balance. The container has been placed on its side with plant material emerging from openings in the top and side. Two stems of Asiatic lilies complete the design.

CREATIVE LINE-MASS

All the general rules and descriptions of a Creative Line design apply as well to the Creative Line-mass design, which is also open form. The only difference is that in this case more plant material is used, resulting in a slight de-emphasis of line. The line itself may follow any of the directions described in the preceding discussion of Creative Line designs.

A stylish, clean-cut Creative Line-mass design. Decorative wood and ting-ting emerge from two different openings in the container; stems of yellow gladiolus and variegated hosta foliage mass to create two focal areas.

CREATIVE MASS

Though these designs share with Creative Line and Creative Line-mass designs the characteristics which allow more than one focal area, the possibility of more than one point of emergence, and some abstraction of plant material, Creative Mass designs are of closed form and never Abstract in concept. They are favored by those who like to use more plant material than is possible in either Creative Line or Creative Line-mass designs. The freedom the designer is allowed—to creatively use larger amounts of plant material and other components—gives more opportunity to create designs that blend with present-day furnishings and architecture.

Enclosed spaces are considered part of the mass, a significant departure from Traditional Mass designs; viewer and designer alike must here learn to regard space differently. Striking contrasts, simplicity, restraint, and a lack of transitional materials are further, distinctly non-Traditional hallmarks of Creative Mass designs. They are often tailored and restrained in effect, using either small amounts of several plant materials or larger amounts of fewer types. Plant material is grouped by like color, form, or type and then massed along lines or spaces created by lines.

In this Creative Mass design, Dutch iris, lilies, and silver tree foliage combine to accent the graceful, sweeping line of the dried branch. The container echoes the color of the branch and foliage. Design by Hallie Brown, Stone Mountain, Georgia.

Two points of emergence and two focal areas play important roles in this Creative Mass design. The decorative wood on the right balances the plant material on the left, which reflects in reverse the form of the wood. The lilies on the lower right provide visual balance. Note that Creative Mass designs are less tightly massed than their Traditional counterparts; the lack of transitional materials heightens the emphasis on spatial relationships.

FRAMED SPATIAL

This is a light, airy design with an unconventional use of plant material and other components. All components are combined into a single, unified design which is then staged within a volume of space defined by a frame, appearing to float in the space created, visually penetrating it. No part of the design should appear to touch the frame; the only connection must be the unseen means of suspension, usually strands of nylon monofilament. Motion is implied, not actual. Often, in addition to being suspended, the design is anchored to the frame on the sides and bottom. Though it must retain its visual separateness, the frame may be unified with the design by repeating one of its colors. In flower show work, the suspended design must be Creative; a Traditional design placed or suspended within a frame does not fit this classification. In the home, a frame will add a special touch to any design.

FREE-STANDING ABSTRACT

This type of arrangement meets all criteria for an Abstract design, often created in or with a non-Traditional container, but does not fall into any of the other Abstract style categories. As with any design that is free-standing—meaning it can be viewed from any side—it is critical that such a design be well balanced and pleasing from every angle.

HANGING

Great space savers, Hanging (or suspended) designs have been popular for many years and are as effective in a commercial building as in a home. For best viewing, they should be hung at eye level or slightly above. They may consist of two or more designs used together to create a single, unified design and may have one or more moving parts. The Hanging design is not a Mobile and has no motorized movement. This classification no longer includes wreaths, swags, kissing balls, or other similar crafts.

Hanging designs are divided into two types. A Type I is created in a container or basket, for example, and is meant to hang still against a flat, solid surface, such as a wall, door, or easel. Type II may move hypnotically as it is freely suspended from a hook in the ceiling, frame, or other structure. In a home interior, these designs are shown to good advantage when suspended from the ceiling or chandelier over a dining or buffet table, in lieu of or coordinated with a table design. Where space is limited, such as in a stairwell or entrance hall, a Hanging design of either type is a splendid solution.

These designs differ from Framed Spatial designs as the Hanging design may have actual motion and staging is not limited to a frame.

Dried, clipped palm—some natural, some sprayed white—creates an architectural pattern of strong vertical and horizontal lines in this Free-standing Abstract. Though it is not apparent in a two-dimensional photo, the relation of line to line changes as one circles the design. Carnations grouped and taped together at their stems appear in two large round forms, and together with the distributed force of the line pattern ensure that interest is equated throughout the design.

ILLUMINARY

Illuminary designs are relatively new and incorporate one or more lights as an integral component of the design; an arrangement which is merely lit by a spotlight for better viewing is not an Illuminary design. The emphasis is on color, pattern, and balance.

Chaser lights, colored lights, lights enclosed in plastic tubing, reflected lights, and other varieties may be used as lines, forms, or other elements within the design. Such lights are often available during the holiday season. Lights may also be incorporated into the background, base, container, underlay, or some other component. In all cases, mechanics—such as batteries, cords, and wires—must be hidden so they do not detract from the design. Suitable lights, although they are often difficult to find, will not be bulky or produce too much heat; the ideal is a long-lived, battery-operated light. Perhaps such lighting will become more commonly available as flower arrangers request it.

In a flower show, the exhibitor must be sure to determine whether the schedule allows lights, and if so, what kind. Be certain also that the lights you have chosen meet all safety codes and are adequately wired. If in doubt, check with the show chairman.

The Construction of tree branches seen earlier, this time combined with lights in plastic tubing for an Illuminary design. A second piece of tubing with stiff wire enclosed has been wound around the illuminated line material so that it holds the desired form. Juniper branches and red and pink carnations complete the design. The electrical cord is out of sight, passing unobtrusively through a slit in the background material.

KINETIC

These are designs of movement, real or implied. All Kinetic designs must be Abstract. To place a design on a turntable does not necessarily make it a Kinetic design; it may move, but it must be Abstract to be a true Kinetic.

There are three types of Kinetic designs: Motorized, Mobiles, and Stabiles. Motorized designs have real movement. They are actually driven by small motors concealed within the arrangement which run programmed movements of the entire design or certain of its parts. It is free-standing and three-dimensional. The entire design may simply be staged to rotate on a turntable, or, more intriguing, a

A mobile by Alexander Calder. *Sea Scape*. 1947. Painted wood, string and metal. 36½ × 60 × 21 inches. (92.7cm × 152.4cm × 53.3cm). Collection of Whitney Museum of American Art. Purchase, with funds from the Howard and Jean Lipman Foundation, Inc.

small motor attached to one or more components may move only that portion of the design in a repetitive fashion.

Mobiles as floral designs are a borrowing from another of the visual arts, an adaptation of the mobiles of artist Alexander Calder. They too are Kinetics with actual motion, here non-mechanized, induced by normal air currents. Mobiles are suspended from the top and have several moving units attached. All components must be light in weight in order to move freely. None of the moving units may touch or be obstructed by another unit, or motion will be lost. Good balance is essential if the parts are to hang and move properly. Visual balance of the whole, as well as within each individual unit, must also be achieved. Individual units are usually two-dimensional, but the change in direction effected by air currents gives the overall design a third dimension.

Dried plant material is often used in Mobiles as it is usually light in weight and requires no moisture. Fresh plant material may be used, but if a constant source of moisture is necessary, problems with balance are inevitable. As the oasis and plant material begin to dry out, imbalance occurs. Balance will also be impaired as moisture is again provided. In both instances, adjustments will have to be made, and re-made, to individual units.

To create a Mobile, some designers begin with the bottom unit and work their way to the top. Others begin with the top piece, from which all units are suspended, and work their way down. Carpet thread is a good material for suspending one unit from another. It is easier to tie than nylon monofilament and will be unobtrusive if a neutral color is used. Small pieces of decorative wood, shells, bits of bark, or any other lightweight material, man-made or natural, may be included along with the plant material in a Mobile.

A Mobile is clearly too time-consuming to make on site and thus presents a challenge to the transporter when it is meant for public exhibition. Once assembled and properly balanced at home, the entire Mobile may be carefully placed against a flat panel of stiff cardboard and each unit individually pinned to it for secure transportation. Alternatively, each individual unit may be fitted into a plastic bag for protection, and the whole Mobile gently settled into a flat box for transport.

People—especially children—are often fascinated by Mobiles, making them excellent exhibits for flower shows or use in public buildings or spaces. If tiny, wrapped packages or other holiday items are incorporated, a Mobile makes an attractive and unusual holiday decoration for the home.

The third sort of Kinetic, a Stabile, is static. Its movement is implied; it does not move but appears capable of movement. It must seem to have been frozen in mid-motion and should look as though movement might begin again at any moment. Stabiles are three-dimensional, free-standing, and, like all Kinetics, Abstract. They are always fixed in place at the base; the anchoring quality of the base or stem of the container may be a contributing factor to the effect of arrested motion. The plant material should contribute to this illusion as well, soaring up into space perhaps, or arranged more toward the horizontal, giving a wind-swept look, for example. However plant material is placed, it should lead the eye rapidly over and through the design.

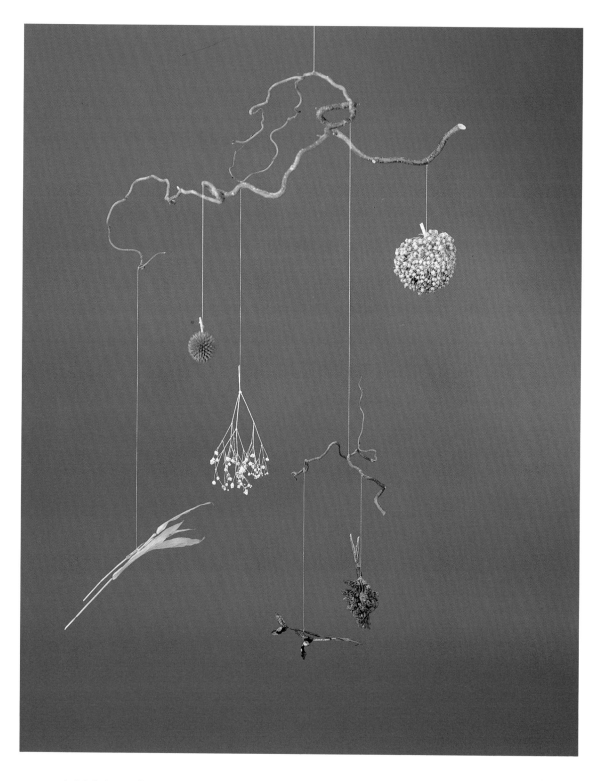

A Mobile as floral art, composed entirely of dried and treated plant material. It has been displayed against a dark background so that the threads so vital to its construction are visible.

A Stabile, with the "movement" of the looped cable—a found object from an abandoned logging site—arrested by the anchor of decorative wood. Stems of gladiolus and clipped fatsia foliage complete the design.

MINIATURE

Miniature designs are small replicas of large designs. They are Creative or occasionally Traditional. In flower show work, the maximum measurement is five inches in each direction: height, width, depth, and any diagonal possible throughout the design. Staging should be in proper proportion; however, backgrounds, frames, niches, or pedestals are not included in the overall dimensions. An arrangement meant for the home is of course not bound by these size restrictions.

Scale and proportion are extremely important in Miniature designs. Generally speaking, the container should be no more than one-third the height or width of the design; a bloom should be no more than one-third the size of the container. As these individual components must be in scale with one another, so must the final design be in proportion to its location. Such tiny designs are best suited for very small spaces, such as a windowsill, ledge, shelf, or tray.

Plant material must be small in size in order to be in scale to the small dimensions of a Miniature design. For those who delight in Miniature designs, a multitude of plants are available in scale. A small corner of the garden can be picturesquely devoted to them and provide a more than adequate supply of plant material for these tiny arrangements. Many plants have dwarf or miniature species or cultivars desirable for their blooms, such as alchemilla, astilbe, chrysanthemum, dianthus, dill, forget-me-not, heath, heather, iris, lily-of-the-valley, saxifrage, rhododendrons, roses, and many of the succulents. Ferns, holly, hosta, ivy, and ornamental grasses are all popular for their foliage. Contorted filbert twigs, grapevine tendrils, or small pieces of decorative wood may provide suitable line material.

Containers for Miniature designs may not be as easy to find, and the arranger must think creatively. A careful look about the house may turn up the lipstick tube, thimble, or especially pretty pill bottle that one often sees in flower show work. A dollhouse dish does nicely as well. A seashell, half a walnut shell, or the cup portion of an acorn are all more natural possibilities.

Stems are typically very small and delicate in Miniature design, and are therefore easily broken and difficult to control. It follows, then, that mechanics will be problematic. A small amount of floral foam may be tucked into some containers; a bit of steel wool or a section of a child's toothbrush, cut to fit, may provide adequate support in others. One of the greatest difficulties is furnishing an adequate supply of moisture in designs using fresh plant material. However these problems are solved, do be sure plant material is well conditioned before use. It may also be helpful to mist the design occasionally.

OP ART

Op Art was very popular in the 1960s, both in the United States and abroad. Using geometric patterns and strong, parallel lines—often in clearly delineated black and white—painters worked to create an optical illusion of movement on their canvasses. They used abstract patterns with carefully controlled variations of line and form. The moiré pattern of watered silk is a familiar example of this type of pattern and gives the same effect of movement. The sensation imparted to the viewer by Op Art may be pleasing or extremely disturbing.

In floral work, an Op Art design must also be Abstract and create an illusion of movement. Because the Op Art effect is difficult to achieve, the design is often created with a background or panel which has been covered with wallpaper, fabric, or a poster in an Op Art pattern. The simplest way to proceed is to choose this background pattern first, then select plant material that will enhance it. Some plant material can be glued directly to the panel; other plant material may be superimposed. The careful repetition and placement of strong, aggressive lines and forms of equal strength and color result in a strangely restless, demanding design. Syncopated rhythm moves the eye through the design and adds to the optical disturbance.

Op Art designs remain a challenging study topic for the advanced designer but are seldom used in homes or flower shows.

PARALLEL

Parallel designs have recently become more popular with florists and designers in Europe and the United States. This style closely resembles a fundamental Japanese design type, the Moribana, in which an Oriental landscape or garden scene is depicted in a low, flat container. Parallel designs have three or more units of strong line, paralleling one another, with open spaces between each unit. Plant material and other components must have a strong directional thrust as well. Units may be of the same length or of varying lengths. Plant material or some other component may be placed at the base of the design to connect the units, achieve visual weight and balance, and unify the design. The container itself may provide the same effects.

Units may be organized in one of four ways. Each may be a combination of several different plant materials, none repeating. Each within itself may be of a single type of plant material, or all may be of the same type of plant material. Finally, one plant material may appear repeated in each of the units in combination with other plant material.

In a Parallel design, all units emerge from what is or appears to be a single container. The container selected must be large enough to accommodate all units and allow adequate space between them. Two or more containers may be stacked or placed against one another, but they must appear to be one. Irregularly stacking oblong or round, flat containers to vary the height at which emerging plant material appears is more creative than using a single, rectangular container and will just as successfully reinforce the linear form of the design.

Parallel units may be horizontal, oblique, vertical, or a combination. Whatever the orientation of the units, their line lengths should be great enough to provide a clearly dominant directional thrust. Large containers are usually needed to adequately space the units of a Parallel design, but they often appear visually heavy. Again, a longer line in one or all of the units will balance the visual weight of the container as well as help delineate the dominant line direction.

When a container is round or square, needleholders are placed to form a triangle from which the units emerge. In a rectangular container, the needleholders may be arranged in a straight line, at an angle, or set apart from each other randomly. Any type of container which will allow the placement of three or more parallel units, adequately spaced, is permissible. Some of the available non-Traditional containers would be effective and very creative.

Though National Council makes no distinctions, simply calling for Parallel designs to be Creative, European designers and some florists have divided Parallel designs into two types: decorative and vegetative.

Three containers have been stacked and glued together for this Parallel design, providing two levels of emergence for plant material. Clear, crackled chips of glass add both interest and visual weight at the base of each unit, but the clear container creates space beneath the other two and assures that the design is not bottom-heavy. The near-white joints and black lines of the vertical equisetum are repeated in the iris and containers; ti leaves placed horizontally connect and unify the three units.

In a decorative Parallel, the placement of plant material is studied and stylized, with little importance placed on conveying an accurate reflection of natural growth habit. Plant material is often arranged as it is in Traditional designs: the smallest, lightest material high in the design, and the largest, heaviest at its base. Other designers choose to abstract the plant material through manipulation and/or placement.

In the vegetative Parallel, the design simulates a section of a garden or wild meadow. Plant material is placed so that natural growth habit is mimicked as closely as possible, with flowers high in the design and stems a more integral part of it, as in nature.

REFLECTIVE

In a Reflective design, components within the design itself actually reflect an image back to the viewer. Whether the image presented is one of the viewers themselves, or lights, objects, and colors within and around the design, a unique and intimate visual connection is created for the viewer. Though some also use a reflective background, the most effective Reflective designs will reemphasize this quality throughout the arrangement by means of additional reflective components. These designs have an inherent capacity to surprise, interest, and delight the viewer. To merely place a design on, or in front of, a mirror misses the mark completely.

SCULPTURAL FORM

A Sculptural Form design is three-dimensional, one in which the plant material remains subordinate. Here, the single-unit sculptured form, either man-made or naturally formed, is dominant and must appear to have been carved, chiseled, or welded together from one type of material. Decorative wood together with a ceramic container may have three dimensions, but it is not a Sculptural Form design because it consists of two materials.

In a flower show, the schedule may specify that the dominant form be made of a certain type of material. Decorative wood, fresh bamboo, or equisetum are often used if the form must be of plant material. If man-made items are permitted, the arranger may choose from glass, mesh, plexiglass, rope, or screen, among other materials. Even a container may itself be the sculptured form. In any case, plant material must be added to enhance the chosen form, though a lesser amount will be required than in most other Creative designs.

It is important that color, size, amount, and placement of the additional plant material be carefully studied, so that the form itself remains properly dominant. A color that is too bright, a form that is too large, too great an amount of plant material, or plant material placed in such a way that it obscures too much of the unit—all will divert attention from the sculptured form and take away from its required dominance.

A Sculptural Form design—suggestive of a Henry Moore sculpture—in which the container provides the dominant form. A single pincushion protea enhances it, hinting at its color and repeating the open space at its center; the dried branch repeats its form. Although tall, the line material is very weak, allowing the container to remain dominant. What would be a fault in another design becomes an asset in a Sculptural Form.

In this less-successful Sculptural Form design, lilies and looped foliage have replaced the protea, thereby weakening the dominance of the featured form. They are arranged in too compact a manner, too close to the container, making proportion and balance a problem. The line appears even weaker, but the container now seems disturbingly heavy. Such problems often arise from a poor selection or combination of components.

With plant material now the clear focus, the design is no longer a Sculptural Form. The mass of lilies and foliage, placed in a more carefree, loose manner, has visually lightened the container, but the weakness of the line is now an undesirable quality. Stronger line material would improve this arrangement.

On the left, two plastic forms—plexiglass and a Tangle™—create a starkly modern Sculptural Form, a study in tension between curved and linear shapes. The design is subtly enhanced by a single clipped palm leaf, painted black, though even gray or very dark green foliage would not have destroyed the required dominance of the form.

On the right, a variant demonstrating the power of small amounts of strong color. Close your eyes briefly, open them, and note which part of the arrangement first attracts your attention. Most people will find their eyes immediately drawn to the small, red form of the grouped carnations. The sculptured form, though much larger in size, is no longer dominant.

SHADOW BOX

In a Shadow Box, a translucent material, such as rice paper, is placed in the foreground, facing the viewer. The design is situated between it and a light source which casts the silhouette of the design onto the paper. Light is a vital element in the creation of a Shadow Box, but as only the shadow of the design will be seen by the viewer, only the form, line, pattern, size, and spaces of the design itself are important. A bold, dramatic, open form design, with interesting use of space, will present a more intriguing shadow than one that is a compact, closed form design. The elements of color and texture and the condition of the plant material remain unseen.

SMALL

Unlike the Miniature design, which requires small-sized plant material, the Small design uses average-sized plant material. In flower show work, the size of the design may be no more than eight inches in any one direction; pedestals, backgrounds, or niches are not included in the overall measurement. As with Miniature designs, scale and proportion are of great importance, both within the design and in its staging. Small designs are sometimes Traditional.

STILL LIFE

In other arts, a still life is a drawing or painting of a grouping of inanimate objects. Some are heavy with symbolism and others are purely decorative, but they all might be said to revolve around a certain theme. Historically, we know that such groupings of objects were incorporated into paintings as far back as Roman times. Dutch and Flemish artists brought the art of the still life to a high degree of perfection, painting such subjects as bouquets of many kinds of flowers with a multitude of accessories. To sketch or paint a still life remains a popular assignment in art classes to this day.

Homemakers and decorators create still lifes unwittingly as they group objects in the home. A reading lamp, book, coaster, and a single rose in a bud vase, arranged on a small table, makes an inviting group of related objects that, taken together, present a theme of comfort, relaxation, and contemplation.

In modern floral design, a Still Life is a grouping of related components and plant material, realistic in feeling and likewise thematically organized. Objects are dominant in the design, and all must be true to normal size and function. This last requirement effectively rules out the use of figurines. A small ceramic duck, for example, would be unacceptable; however, a duck decoy, because it is life-size, might be included in a Still Life with an appropriate theme—"Before the Hunt," for example. Objects may be included for their color, form, size, and texture as well, but must always somehow assist in the interpretation of the theme or the telling of the story.

A Still Life is usually staged on a table, or a portion of a table. In flower shows, a background, niche, or frame is sometimes part of the staging as well.

Plant material—whether flowers, foliage, fruits, or vegetables—may be attached to these areas of the staging, placed in related groupings on the table, or otherwise arranged as dictated by the principles of design. If kept out of water, plant material must be long-lasting. Often, water picks or orchid tubes provide the necessary moisture. Though plant material is required, it is not restricted to a container; a Still Life in flower show work never contains a complete flower arrangement.

A Still Life differs from an Assemblage, as the Assemblage must be Abstract, need not be interpretive, and depends upon the combination of *unrelated* objects and plant material.

SYNERGISTIC

Synergy is a combined or cooperative action or force. A Synergistic design is made up of several parts which, taken together, have a greater total visual impact than the sum of their individual effects.

A Synergistic design must have at least three parts or groupings, though it may have more; it is not the same as a pair of designs. Plant material, containers, and other components share common characteristics and create an artistic whole when used in combination. Each part or grouping contributes to this effect of wholeness as each is related to the others by color, form, repetition, or plant material. A connective, some component that actually leads from one grouping to another, may be of assistance in unification.

The designer may begin by creating individual designs—each in its own container and each complete within itself—and then combine them all into a unified design. The alternative is to assemble the containers and create the whole design without conscious regard to the designs which unfold in each container.

Sometimes a designer chooses to leave one container empty, but unless there were three other containers of plant material, this would be risky in a flower show. When only three containers are used and one is left without plant material, the judges may not consider it a true Synergistic design of three parts. This is not to say that one cannot leave a container empty; just be sure at least three containers contain plant material.

TRANSPARENCY

Around the middle of the 20th century, a three-dimensional design type developed which required the viewing of some components through others. Transparencies make extensive use of overlapping forms which greatly increases the appearance of the design's third dimension: depth. The technique of overlapping has of course been a part of good design from the beginning, but never before was it required that some components be seen through others.

Components may be of transparent material, such as acrylic, glass, grillwork, mesh, open-weave fabric, plexiglass, or screen. Some natural material lends itself to this sort of design as well, such as bare branches, sea fans, or skeletonized leaves. Lights, focused at several angles, may add to the illusion of depth, which in turn heightens the viewer's sensation of seeing through the design.

Taken alone, no part of this Synergistic design would make a significant statement, but the repetition of plant material, color, container style, and connective work together to create a unified arrangement of great interest. Design by Hallie Brown.

Heliconia abstractly arranged with black vine in an Underwater design. The upside-down heliconia bloom is submerged, a watery reverse-image reflection of the one that rises above it. Clear, crackled glass chips add texture and visual weight to two of the stacked glass-block containers and are interestingly magnified through the third. The yellow background is a perfect complement to the tropical heliconia, which is native to warm, sunny climates.

UNDERWATER

These designs are related to the Underwater designs of Ikebana and to a custom of our Victorian ancestors, who often placed a single bloom under water in a glass ball. Today's Underwater designs submerge only a part or parts of the arrangement, not the entire design. There is no rule as to what portion of the design should be out of water and what portion should be submerged; the amounts are dictated only by the design principle of proportion.

If a round container is used, special attention must be paid to the scale of those materials chosen for submersion because they will be magnified by the water. A square-sided container does not magnify, although sometimes distortion may be observed at its corners. Magnification of size, when it does occur, is a point of great interest in these designs. Clear, transparent containers are generally better than those in which the glass is tinted; with a clear container, underwater components will be easily visible, which is usually what the designer intends. A colored glass container may work for or against a design, depending upon the desired effect.

Plant material must have hard surface qualities, or it will quickly become waterlogged—a result which should be avoided at all costs. Plant material in such a state is most unattractive. Some of the more exotic tropicals, such as anthurium, birds-of-paradise, and heliconia, resist waterlogging very well. More commonly available plant material, such as lilies or evergreen foliage, whether needled or thickly textured, would also suit. Citrus fruits, such as lemons, limes, and oranges, do well because of their oily, water-repellent rinds. It is wise to experiment with selected plant materials before using them in a design that will require submersion for more than a few hours.

Mechanics may be tricky since they are magnified along with the plant material. A small needleholder, firmly attached to the bottom of the container, may work well if plant material is to emerge upward from that point. Select the smallest possible needleholder and make sure the clay adhering to the bottom is not visible. If plant material will extend downward from the mouth of the container, plumber's lead or fisherman's pencil-lead may be used to secure it. Both materials are very flexible and can be shaped around stems, then bent over the rim of the container for support. If a portion of the plant material emerges from the rim and leads upward in the design, this same method works well. In any case, make sure all ends are tidily concealed in the completed design. These designs need not be made in a single container; some plant material may be submerged in one container and another part of the design placed in another. Making a complete design in the bottom of the container and another on top of the container misses the challenge of the Underwater design and is unacceptable.

In the actual assembly of the design, plant material should be positioned first, then water added. If done in the reverse, tiny bubbles will cover the plant material, and it will be much more difficult to place the components. If the container is very large, the design must be in place—that is, in its final position at the exhibit or the home—before water is added, as it will be very heavy when filled. Eventually a siphon can be used to remove the water. Water should come to the rim of the container, unless there is some reason, based on the principles of design or the theme of the particular design, which would justify creating a water line across the arrangement.

It is vital that upon completion, all materials, both under water and out, have the appearance of a unified design. Creativity is a must if the design is to be a success.

VIBRATILE

A Vibratile is an Abstract design which gives off vibrations of sound and/or motion. By actually touching the arrangement or an indicated part of it, the viewer participates in creating a motion or sound—or both. Some Vibratiles have a constantly moving component which may or may not produce a sound as a result of the motion. Again, the viewer is drawn in by the fascination of moving parts, especially when accompanied by sound. All components, moving or not, even the selected sound-making devices, must contribute in some integral way to the design as a whole. Bells, dried seed pods, whistles, and wind chimes are all sound-producing objects; the creative designer will think of others. The sound generated must never be annoying.

VIGNETTE

Sometimes referred to as a "Slice of Life," a Vignette in flower show terminology refers to a full-scale recreation of a small portion of a room, complete with furniture, draperies, paintings, and so on. Unlike the Still Life, the Vignette includes an entire floral design in some natural way, and all components—not just those within the floral arrangement—must relate to one another in some way, whether by style, color, texture, or period. Because they show both the art of floral design and a possible setting for it, Vignettes are popular features of holiday shows and may include a Christmas tree, wreath, or other holiday decoration.

Though we do not label them as such, Vignettes are created in every home as we arrange furniture, centerpieces, and other appointments to create an attractive and pleasant surrounding for family and guests.

As has been seen, a number of clearly defined rules govern the category of even Creative designs in flower show work. Notwithstanding these strictures—which must be looked upon as the necessary challenges of the art form—it is up to the designer to use his or her ingenuity and inventiveness, guided always by both personal taste and the principles of design, to assemble a Creative design that is truly a work of floral art.

9 Beyond the Centerpiece: Table Settings

The desire to create a centerpiece for one's own dining table was the original impetus for many flower arrangers, who then went on to make a lifelong study of the art and its infinite possibilities. Quite simple or most elegant—and often both—a beautifully set table, because of the obvious care the arranger took in designing it, communicates a feeling of graciousness and warmth to those fortunate enough to gather around it, adding distinction and a heightened sense of celebration to any occasion. In this enlightened, health-conscious age, much focus is put on the foods we choose and how they are prepared, but the presentation of the final product must not be forgotten. An attractive table setting can add much to our enjoyment of both the food and the company.

Whether a table setting is intended for the pleasure of our family and guests or as a competitive entry in a flower show, careful coordination of all its components is essential. The table appointments—cloth, dinnerware, glassware, and other items—should appear to be an extension of the mood of the space in which they are staged. They may reflect a natural, colorful theme for meals staged alfresco, or may echo the elegant formality, casual informality, or sleek modernity of an interior design. Slavishly following the prevailing style of a room allows for little variation, and many find this boring. An occasional departure from the expected is not only acceptable, but desirable. Table settings are often eclectic, combining appointments from more than one period.

Ours is a mobile society, and table appointments that perfectly complemented our last home may not suit the present home as well. If dinnerware seems too casual for the current dining area, entertaining in a buffet style might be a better alternative than a sit-down dinner, making informal dinnerware once again appropriate.

There are varying degrees of formality, from very formal to very casual. Formal dining, in the strictest sense, is rarely seen today, confined mostly to official government functions or society events staffed with competent professional servers. The great majority of us dine day-to-day in a more informal or casual manner, with only an occasional semi-formal event.

The nature of an event together with the time of day it is held often helps set

147

the tone or degree of formality. Evening events are more likely to be formal or semi-formal, breakfasts and luncheons, informal or casual. As with any general rule, there will be exceptions, such as the more formal bridal luncheon or a relaxed evening barbecue. Trust common sense and good taste to settle any questions you may have in judging the right note of formality to strike in a particular table setting.

Setting a beautiful table requires more careful planning than designing a single floral arrangement because more variables are involved. We will consider each of these components individually but will first discuss generally how they all are best brought together.

First, let us set the stage. The table top is the designer's frame of reference, the space within which all components are arranged. Occupied and unoccupied space must be proportionately pleasing; it may be helpful to mentally divide the table into quadrants to check for balance and proportion. Too many settings or too many components create a cluttered look and make dining difficult.

For a coordinated setting, all table appointments must be harmoniously related. The decorative unit—which is not necessarily in the center of the table, and therefore not always a centerpiece!—includes a flower arrangement and possibly candles and an accessory; all must be related to one another as well as to the table appointments in color, texture, and style. Very fine china, dainty stemware, sterling silver, and finely textured linen table coverings demand a type of flower design and candle in the decorative unit that is different from the type demanded by earthenware, coarse fabric, heavy glassware, and stainless flatware. Roses or camellias and tall, thin tapers would be appropriate for use with the first setting, but totally at odds with the second. Even allowing for some degree of variability, a very creative black-and-white design is too far removed from a traditional china pattern with a narrow band of dainty, pastel flowers to be used in conjunction with it.

Color plays a vital role in the early stages of planning and coordinating table components. One of the colors in the room's decor will usually be repeated in the place plate. The coordinating color does not have to be the dominant color in the room, as this may prove monotonous. Better to choose a subordinate color, one used less often in the room. A color picked up from a painting, the draperies, a patterned carpet, or the upholstery often provides the most successful unifying element.

As discussed earlier, the effects of color are powerful, and they are no less so when included in a table setting. Black and white are dramatic; with the addition of red, the three colors communicate excitement. Green and white are soothing, cooling colors, and a monochromatic harmony is very subtle. These qualities translate to a table setting as well as they do to a floral design.

The effects of light and its influence on color must also be taken into account when planning a table setting, as the colors in plant material as well as those which appear on the dishes and table coverings will be affected. Incandescent light and candles—both of which have yellow undertones—will make blue and violet seem to disappear, but red, yellow, and orange will appear more brilliant than usual in such a cast. Blue and violet are better selections when lit by natural light and therefore better for a luncheon, where artificial lighting would not be required.

Though color and pattern may be contributing factors, the degree of formality (and by inference, the quality of the coordinating components) is often more closely related to texture than to any other single element. The finer the texture, the more formal the element; items which are rough in texture—hand-woven mats, baskets, pottery and the like—are more informal. This notion applies even to the choice of plant material: think of the smoothness of the elegant calla lily versus the rougher bloom of the countrified marigold. The texture of table coverings and dinnerware will help set the tone for the choice of remaining components. Though most components should be of a similar texture, creating dominance, a contrasting texture must be included to avoid monotony.

Bright, vivid color combinations are often casual or informal; the neutral colors of black, white, and gray contribute to a more formal mood. For example, earthenware plates patterned with bright orange poppies are fit for a casual or informal setting, whereas a sophisticated black-and-white pattern on fine china imparts an elegant formality, an almost black-tie effect, to the occasion.

COMPONENTS

Dinnerware

The selection of a dinnerware pattern is too important to be made in haste. Because of its size and repetition, dinnerware is the most dominant component in the overall setting and should coordinate in some way with the room and furnishings. Choose a pattern that will be pleasing and versatile over a long period of time. Of course, uniquely patterned sets, such as those decorated with a Christmas tree motif, are appropriate and lovely for their particular season.

A great deal of variety is easily accomplished if two carefully chosen sets are at the designer's disposal; if selected with the first set in mind, a second set may be purchased to augment the possibilities of the set already on hand. A floral pattern, for example, may blend well with a plate of a complementary single color or one with a solid-colored band, allowing the two to be used together in several variations. The patterned dinner plate might be combined with the banded salad plate, or vice versa. For a dinner party, the designer might choose plain banded plates for the men and floral ones for the women, resulting in a very pleasing pattern of alternation around the table. One hostess, whose favorite flower is the rose, collected single place settings of varying rose patterns, yet all of a similar quality and formality; she sets a luncheon table for six—each with a different rose pattern, all repeated in a decorative unit of mixed roses—which is simply smashing.

Coordination between plates with a floral pattern and the decorative unit is usually most successful when the same type of flowers are included in the floral design. Rose-patterned plates look best with a decorative unit which includes roses; a china pattern of calla lilies is most effective when paired with a dramatic arrangement of callas. If several different flowers appear on the plate, it is not necessary to repeat each one.

Dinnerware with a wide colored border or a gold or silver band may be more easily combined with a variety of flowers. A fruit pattern is charming when used in a design of fruits alone or in combination with flowers and/or foliage.

A visit to any china department will reveal the myriad choices in dinnerware available to today's designer, with wide variations of pattern, quality, and affordability. China or porcelain is fine-textured, hard, non-porous, shiny, smooth, and translucent. Hold a plate to the light: good china will allow the silhouette of the hand to be seen through it. Because it is fired at a very high temperature, china is more resistant to chipping than other types of dinnerware. Fine china is always used for formal and semi-formal dining; very formal dining rooms seem to demand dinnerware of such high quality and traditional pattern.

Earthenware, stoneware, and pottery are coarse-textured, heavy, opaque, and more easily chipped than china. A wide range of quality and many patterns are available, ranging from very smooth, plain, and tailored to highly decorated and very casual. A few high-quality plastics, perfect for informal dining such as picnics or barbecues, are also available; paper products are acceptable only for the most casual gatherings.

Dinnerware may be purchased in a complete set or by place settings. A place setting usually includes a dinner plate, salad plate, soup bowl/plate, and cup and saucer. When setting a table, include whichever pieces are required by the planned menu. The menu itself may also be a determining factor in the final choice of dinnerware and is definitely something to consider when planning a particular table setting. For example, a semi-formal setting of a traditional gold-edged pattern does nothing to enhance the presentation of hamburgers, baked beans, and potato salad. In the same way, a fresh fruit salad would appear to much better advantage on a bright pink or purple plate than would a breakfast of herbed eggs, ruddy bacon, and hash browns.

When the decisions have been made and the table is ready for setting, one must place the appointments carefully and neatly. The dinner plate is placed approximately one inch from the edge of the table. Allow between twenty and twenty-four inches from the center of one place setting to the center of the next. If dinnerware has a non-repetitive pattern, fix on a certain element in the pattern and place all pieces in the same manner, orienting them as if the plate were the face of a clock: all clusters of cherries at two o'clock, for instance. Of course, if a pattern of a single, centered element is used, plates should be arranged so that the diner will view it as it was meant to be seen: with a flower, for instance, stem down, bloom up. Bread and butter plates, if included in the place setting, are set on the left, above the forks. The soup bowl or plate is set on the place plate; a rimmed soup plate is the preference for formal or semi-formal dining. If salad is served as a separate course, the salad plate is set on the place, or service, plate; if salad is served along with the main course, it is placed to the left of the forks. Cups and saucers are almost always on a breakfast table, but usually not on a dinner table until dessert is served. In either instance, the cup and saucer is placed on the right, at about the two o'clock position.

Flatware

Eating utensils, flat or otherwise, may be referred to generally as flatware and may be of silverplate, sterling silver, stainless steel, or other man-made materials. Many traditional patterns are available, some centuries old, along with creative new designs which may incorporate both gold and silver, colored handles, or other unusual features. Quality and pattern should coordinate with other table appointments. Good balance, pleasing proportions, and comfortable weight are additional criteria for selection.

Flatware should be neatly spaced approximately one inch from the edge of the table. Forks are placed on the left of the plate—in order of use—from the outside toward the plate. The knife is placed on the right, next to the plate, with the cutting edge toward the plate. Spoons are placed to the right of the knife, again in order of use, from the outside toward the plate. If a bread and butter plate is used, the butter knife is placed horizontally on the edge of the butter plate furthest from the diner, with the cutting edge placed forward. Because of the risk of theft, flatware is never included in table exhibits in a flower show, but disposable plastic utensils or inexpensive wooden chopsticks are sometimes permitted.

Table coverings

Table coverings—cloths, place mats, and runners—are optional, sometimes missing altogether, sometimes layered or used in varying combinations. Whenever they are employed, however, they are a most important part of the table setting. As they create the background for all components, they must be compatible in every respect. If the tabletop is lovely to see—of acrylic, glass, marble, or an exceptional wood, for example—and will not be damaged by heat or stains, it is not necessary to use table coverings at all. Their use then becomes a matter of taste, and the designer may include them or not, as desired.

Whether they are required to perform a strict function or not, table coverings in their various forms are by far the easiest and least expensive way to vary table settings. The wise designer will therefore take advantage of the wide assortment available to stock the linen closet at home.

Place mats, offered in the most bewildering array of materials, shapes, and styles, are often combined with tablecloths or runners for an up-to-date look. They may be oblong, oval, round, or fan-shaped; of fabric, glass, plexiglass, or vinyl; solid-colored, patterned, or reflective; delicately fine-textured or coarsely hand-woven. Consider all the options, never failing to relate color, pattern, quality, and texture to other table appointments.

Round mats that drape well may be positioned to hang slightly over the edge of the table; place mats of other shapes are placed approximately one-half inch from the edge of the table. Ideally, all items in the place setting should be arranged on the mat; if size does not permit, place all items as close to the mat as possible so that there is no question of their belonging to that place setting.

If the china is patterned, a plain tablecloth or place mat is preferable; with plain china, a patterned table covering may be more effective. Too much pattern or the combination of too many patterns will create confusion and destroy unity.

Often one of the colors in the dinnerware is repeated in the table covering; white cloths may be dyed to match the desired color if it is an unusual shade. Even more creatively, if one is handy with a sewing machine, the delightful materials available in fabric shops can be combined into unique pieces. A simple net overcloth, properly edged, adds a touch of elegance, and many cloths with metallic threads beautifully complement gold- or silver-banded china, adding distinction to a table set for a special occasion.

The tablecloth overhang is generally from twelve to eighteen inches; on a formal or semi-formal table, approximately eighteen inches is preferred. Insufficient overhang appears skimpy, but an overhang that is too long is an annoyance to the seated guest. On buffet, reception, tea, or wedding head tables, the overhang is usually to the floor. An underlay may be used to the floor, with a cloth of another color placed over it in a proportionate overhang. The underlay may be white or any color that will complement the table covering; do not overlook its potential as another avenue to strengthen color coordination among the table appointments.

Napkins

Napkins are included on all tables. On formal or semi-formal tables, they should match or blend with the cloth. For more casual settings, they may match, blend, or even contrast with the cloth or mat. If the cloth or mat is patterned, napkins in a solid color will usually be best; often the napkins will repeat one of the colors in the decorative unit or plate pattern. Two napkins of different colors may be used at each place setting to further coordinate and develop a color harmony.

Napkins which are purchased in matching sets are sized appropriately for the tablecloth or mat ensemble of which they are a part. Often in more casual sets—for instance, coupled with a pattern that would do well for a luncheon table—one finds the napkins are sized slightly smaller than those found on a dinner table, but it is not a requirement that luncheon napkins be smaller than dinner napkins. Napkin holders are often employed and should be coordinated with other components, as they too are available in many types and a wide range of quality.

Within the table setting, the designer may position the napkin in a variety of ways: in the center of the service plate, to the left of the service plate, or in a glass or goblet, depending upon the formality of the occasion. On formal or semi-formal tables, placement in the center of the plate or to its left is preferred, as is the traditional, oblong fold of the napkin. Napkins may be folded in many other more creative ways, another of the special touches that render a table setting pleasing and unique. Entire books have been devoted to the subject, and a department store's linen department, which may incorporate creatively folded napkins in its displays, is often a good visual resource. The gracious designer will avoid styles which are difficult to unfold.

Glassware

Glassware or crystal may include tumblers, water goblets, wine glasses, or dessert plates or bowls. The color, pattern, and degree of formality should be linked in some way to the dinnerware. Clear crystal sometimes seems to disappear from view on the table; colored crystal is often a better choice. Formal to semi-formal dining usually means tall, delicate stemware; for less formal settings, glassware may range from the stemware just described to styles with shorter stems or no stem at all. The water goblet is placed directly above the knife and spoons, with the wine goblet to its right.

Candles

Candles may be used on any table—even the breakfast table—if they fit the occasion. They add the same degree of charm to the setting of a wedding party breakfast or birthday brunch as they do to the dinner table, where they are most often found. As a general rule, the more formal the table, the more slender the candles. On a semi-formal table, such tapers might be used in a tall candelabrum which incorporates a floral design as well, the whole making up the decorative unit.

Candles may serve many purposes in a table setting besides adding beauty, elegance, and atmosphere; they may lend necessary height to a design or help portray a theme or carry out a color harmony. Candles too are available in many colors, sizes, and styles, all aspects to be considered when making a selection. Slow-burning candles are preferable and may be added to a design singly, in pairs, or indeed in any desired number. Varying the heights of the candles helps create interest, but remember that the candle flames should be either above or below the eye level of the seated guests.

Accessories

Accessories are sometimes used in a table setting. Never a mere after-thought or something added only to fill space, an accessory must make a major contribution to the design of which it is a part, such as interpreting the theme or carrying the color scheme a step further. As is true for all elements in a table set-ting, accessories must relate in color, style, and texture to other components. Lovely crystal figures would be most appropriate in an elegant setting; some-thing more casual, like a large seashell or glass fishing float, might be a welcome addition to a seafood luncheon table, for example. Whatever the occasion, the accessory must always be in good taste.

Decorative unit

The decorative unit is the floral design or designs that grace the table, pos-sibly in conjunction with candles and/or accessories. Proportion and scale of the design as it relates to the table are most important: the floral arrangement should occupy no less than one-fourth and no more than one-third of the table surface. It is vital that plant material be fastidiously clean and well groomed, as guests will have a close-up view of the design. Arrange the flowers while seated or at least be sure to view the completed design from a seated position. The relation of viewer to design can make a tremendous difference in its appeal.

For formal or semi-formal settings, the decorative unit is a "centerpiece," literally placed in the center of the table. On other tables, the decorative unit may be placed wherever it is most effective. Whatever its position, it must never inter-fere with dining or conversation among family or guests. Aim for a design which is low enough to see over or around, tall enough to see under, or airy enough to see through.

Container

The container for the decorative unit must relate not only to the plant material and the design style, as mentioned earlier, but to all other components of the table setting as well. In other words, a bean pot of heavy pottery would do well not only because the flowers arranged in it are simple and the design itself informal, but also because it is surrounded by earthenware dishes and casual glassware, is atop a rough-textured, hand-woven runner, and is regarded by guests who have assembled for an informal get-together.

Coordinating the components

The prospect of coordinating so many components may seem daunting at first and perhaps too complicated. One should not be discouraged, however; practice will lead to many successful combinations. A worthwhile exercise is to gather together a sampling of all available table coverings, candles, dinnerware, glassware, and napkins. With everything on hand at once, experiment with dif-ferent combinations to determine which are most pleasing. With this accomplished—certain colors, sizes, and textures now definite—it is easier to decide which container, design style, and plant material will be suitable. This activity may also make clear what is lacking: it may suddenly become obvious that the lovely shade of violet in the banded plates is never quite picked up in any available napkin. A simple purchase can remedy the situation, and a more beauti-ful table is the result.

FUNCTIONAL TABLES

Functional tables are those we encounter in our daily life, arranged for the actual service and/or consumption of food, and several different types will be considered and described here in turn. They do, however, make popular exhibits in many flower shows as well—perhaps because viewers relate easily to table settings, which they have created in their own homes or seen in different social situations.

The exhibitor who is preparing a Functional table setting for a flower show must carefully consider all the qualities we have discussed in order to successfully select, combine, and coordinate its components—with the exception of flatware, which as we have said is excluded for the sake of protecting the exhibitor's valuable possessions. All general flower show policies of the sponsoring organization will also apply to table settings.

In flower show work, the schedule will usually provide the following information: a class title, the occasion for which the table is being set, the number of place settings required, and perhaps even the pieces required in each setting. The height, length, and width of the table must always be specified. Expect the flower show committee to provide the underlay or skirting of the table, but the schedule should verify that this is the case and should also give the color of the cloth that will be used. Beyond these requirements, the fewer restrictions placed on the exhibitor, the better; too many restrictions limit creativity. The exhibitor must use good judgment and logic in planning a table for a flower show. For instance, a Functional table might be set for one, but such a table would hardly be placed in a niche or against a background. It would be very unpleasant to dine in such a setting.

Any of the following types may be included in a flower show, as either Functional or Exhibition settings, as will be explained.

Alfresco

When one attends a picnic, barbecue, tailgate party—or indeed any occasion when food is served out-of-doors—one is dining alfresco, literally "in the cool." Service may be semi-formal, informal, or very casual, with guests sitting or standing, and the table appointments are selected accordingly. Fine china and crystal are perfectly appropriate for a wedding reception staged on the grounds of a country club or patio at home; plastic or paper might be just as suitable for a casual buffet luncheon by the pool. The decorative unit, besides being in keeping with the formality of the occasion, must be exceptionally stable. Avoid candles unless the holder is quite heavy and the flame can be protected from sudden gusts of wind.

Buffet

Because the buffet table does not require space for seating around the table, it may be placed against a wall or window—or anywhere that allows guests to move past in an orderly fashion. A buffet table is usually informal in character; however, some formal functions may have buffet service, utilizing fine china, crystal, and silver. For very casual occasions, plastic or paper plates are sometimes used. Be sure they are sturdy enough to remain rigid when food is placed on them.

Whatever the degree of formality, the placement of the decorative unit must never interfere with the self-service of food. Table appointments as well should be

A Functional table set for an intimate dinner for two. A white underlay and placemat and a black tablecloth establish the sophisticated color scheme and are coordinated with white dinnerware and crystal glassware with black stems. White calla lilies and dark green foliage arranged in an Oriental container complement the green and white napkin rings—and even the folds of the napkins themselves. The goblets reflect the white placemat, adding another point of interest.

placed with ease of service to the guests in mind. Leave adequate space for the placement of serving dishes and avoid overcrowding. Many find that napkins and flatware are most sensibly situated where they may be picked up last. Napkins should be folded so that they are easy to pick up and carry.

There are several ways to serve a buffet meal. In one common method, guests serve themselves and then find their own seating, often holding their plates on their laps or on small tray tables. In this case, a floral design is necessary only on the buffet table.

A more comfortable method involves the same self-service, but guests sit for dining at several smaller tables set for four to eight people. In this instance, there should be a small design on each table, appropriately scaled, as well as a larger one on the buffet table. In another variant, if everyone can be comfortably accommodated at a single table, a decorative unit may be placed on what is in essence a dining table set for a regular sit-down dinner. In both cases, the design on each dining table should be coordinated with the design on the buffet.

Reception

A reception table is similar in many ways to a buffet table. It too may be either formal or informal; in either case, the tablecloth may extend to the floor. Table appointments are arranged symmetrically if formal and asymmetrically if informal; again, they are arranged with ease of service in mind. Table appointments and the decorative unit are selected and arranged in accordance with the formality of the setting.

Semi-formal

Semi-formal and formal tables are in every way closely related. Both require that the decorative unit be placed in the center of the table, and each must include an even number of symmetrically arranged place settings. The main difference is that formal tables require professional servers and are not included in flower show work sponsored by National Council.

A formal place setting usually includes a service plate, bread and butter plate, and one or more wine glasses; the place setting for a semi-formal table may or may not include these items. Linens are usually white, ecru, or pastel; bright colors and patterned cloths may be used only with semi-formal tables.

Informal

At an informally set table, one dines without ceremony. There are no strict rules as to the number of diners or the placement of the decorative unit. Place mats and/or runners are often used instead of tablecloths. The floral design or designs may be variously positioned. One design may be at the back of the table or suspended from the ceiling or chandelier. Two designs are sometimes used, one at each end of the table, and sometimes very small designs are included at each place setting.

Trays

Whether a special indulgence for those in need of pampering or a necessity for the infirm, breakfast or TV trays are meant to be carried, so all components, including the floral design, must be very stable. Space is limited and all components must be small in scale. In preparing a tray, avoid a cluttered look by including only the essentials. Harmony of color and texture is also important. The completed service should be bright and cheerful, especially if meant for one who is ill.

EXHIBITION TABLES

Another type of table—one strictly for flower shows—is the Exhibition table. Its purpose is to illustrate the correlation between table components. Functional considerations are put aside; rather the Exhibition table is a study of form, innovatively staged in such a way as to provide a pleasing overall effect. Exhibition tables are still table settings, requiring that all components, except for those items used in staging, be suitable for use when food is served; these are not groupings of unrelated objects. As with all flower show work, exhibitors must abide by the schedule, yet draw upon their own reserves of taste and imagination.

There are two types of Exhibition tables, which the following guidelines govern equally. Each must include both plant material and components related to dining. The Type I Exhibition table is distinguished by its inclusion of a floral design that is complete in itself—one that would be effective even if it were removed from its setting in the exhibit. The Type II Exhibition table requires the inclusion of plant material, but not in a floral design as such. The only difference between the two is in the way plant material is used.

The schedule must furnish the exhibitor with the measurements of the space that will be allotted for the exhibit; this is essential because all components must be artistically arranged within this space. Space is assigned in several ways. The exhibitor may be allotted a space of certain dimensions on a larger table top that will accommodate several exhibits. Smaller individual tables, such as Parsons or coffee tables, may be provided. An assignment may even consist of nothing more than a prescribed amount of floor space, allowing the exhibitor to use any type of staging desired. The schedule may also determine the occasion for which the setting is planned and around which a theme may be developed, such as an anniversary dinner, an after-the-opera buffet, or a child's birthday party. The formality of the setting should be left to the good judgment of the exhibitor; remember, however, that National Council's *Handbook for Flower Shows* does not include formal tables.

The exhibitor must be allowed to determine the components. Items selected should all relate somehow to the occasion even though they might not be provided in such quantities—or even appear at the same time during the service—if the table were Functional. For instance, the selection may include a cup and saucer as well as a goblet, or two plates and only one goblet. Choosing components for an Exhibition table is not as restrictive as choosing those for a Functional table, as items are selected for color, form, and texture, not function.

Though the Exhibition table is ultimately an exercise in imaginative staging, sometimes the schedule will call for the specific use of a background, frame, or niche. If staging is provided by the flower show committee, its size and color must be described in the schedule. The exhibitor must utilize the allotted space to the best advantage, avoid overcrowding, and always bear in mind the principles of design.

The most creative work will result if the schedule simply specifies "staged in an innovative manner." Boxes, Constructions, picnic baskets, panels, racks, shelving, or step stools are among the possibilities; both plexiglass and wood are popular materials. Some components may be raised using small boxes, bases, or stands; the same result is accomplished more creatively by stacking or suspension. A plate is often displayed on a plate stand; cups and goblets may be on their sides, upside down, or suspended.

A Type I Exhibition table incorporating the decorative unit that graced the preceding Functional table setting. The complete floral design is combined with an abstract form of decorative wood attached inside a frame. Again, white napkins mimic the form of the calla lilies and are placed to create color balance, color pattern, and rhythm.

Another Type I Exhibition table, this time using a Traditional design in combination with a white plate and crystal stemware. The gold that rims the glasses is a deeper echo of the iris beards and a lighter version of the container's color. Napkins repeat the lovely green of the lilac buds. The white iris placed with the crystal assures a smooth, rhythmic flow throughout the setting.

Thanksgiving is the theme for this Type I Exhibition table. The turkey pattern on the dinnerware is repeated in the container, and their colors and textures—as well as those found in the candle, holder, napkin, wood plate, and glassware—are repeated in the arrangement of ornamental grasses and chrysanthemums. Design by Deen Day Smith.

This table setting could be categorized as either Type I or Type II because the entire design—including the round frame—would make a dramatic arrangement for an informal table, especially if several thick yellow candles were included. At top, the stems of yellow gladiolus and clipped yellow-edged foliage follow the split line of the manzanita branch, penetrating the space created by the frame—but placed high enough to allow diners to see one another and converse. At bottom, a contrastingly square black plate, black goblet, yellow napkin, and a bit of the yellow-variegated foliage have been grouped in a unifying blend of repetition and balance.

In this Type II Exhibition table, a single red anthurium enhances the black Tangle™ suspended from the frame with nylon monofilament. Napkins echo the form and color of the anthurium, and their placement pulses with rhythm, leading the viewer's eye through the design. A mug and salad plate carry out the bright color harmony. The built-in square provides an interesting division of the frame's space; its form is densely repeated by the square black plate, which in turn contrasts with the colorful round salad plate. Curves of black goblets, echoing the Tangle™, complete the design.

A background, frame, or niche creates a frame of reference, and this space demands to be creatively employed. One or more frames may be used as staging, with components placed inside, atop, or suspended from the frame using nylon monofilament. Napkins may be attached to a background or niche, or placed over the edge of a frame. The tablecloth may be folded or draped over a portion of the top of the frame, down its front, and continue over the edge of the table. Be very careful to follow the schedule to the letter: "within a frame" means all components must be inside the frame; "using a frame" or "incorporating a frame" allows components to be on or outside the frame. The same holds true with the use of a background; be sure you understand and adhere to the wording of the schedule. The design should extend forward and back outside the narrow depth of the frame in order to create proper third dimension. Avoid the common error of using only the bottom portion of a large space. The creative division and use of space is vital.

Because the Type II Exhibition table does not require a complete floral design, staging may be even more innovative. These exhibits are closely related to the Still Life design described in the previous chapter insofar as the use of plant material is concerned. At their most creative, they are reminiscent of settings sometimes seen in advertisements or store displays. The object of the Type II Exhibition table is to create a single, unified, overall design suggesting the correlation of table components and plant material. Plant material is not restricted to a container, however; it may be placed on the table, background, frame, or niche, or suspended within the allotted space, in any position indicated by the principles of design. Only the amount required for the desired effect should be included; several pieces may be needed to accomplish this, but often the inclusion is as subtle as a single flower, leaf, or branch. Water picks may be used to supply water for plant material requiring it as long as they are hidden from view in the scheme of the design or become an active part of the design.

In staging a Type II table, paper plates, napkins, and other components might be attached to a panel hung on a wall or suspended from the ceiling. Plate hangers may be used to attach other types of dinnerware to a background or niche—be sure all is secure before using your best china! Staging must always be in good taste and is limited only by the flower show schedule and the imagination of the designer.

The Collage seen earlier is used here as background and staging for a Type II Exhibition table. An unusual plate repeats the colors and textures of the Collage. A smoky goblet, yellow lilies, yellow napkin, and blue background further coordinate the setting.

The Assemblage seen earlier provides the background and staging for another Type II Exhibition table. High-quality plastic dinnerware repeats the colors found in the Assemblage. The napkin, goblet, and plates are arranged with asymmetrical balance in mind.

In this variant, the same components, with an additional napkin, have been placed in a more formal arrangement. The napkin folds and their placements, in particular, illustrate static balance.

A Creative design combining multiple stems of equisetum bent into geometric forms which complement the heliconia. The container is very bold in form, demanding an equally bold design.

10 Developing Creativity

Creativity is not a precious quality limited to the favored few. Everyone is born with creative potential, but seldom is that native ability developed to its fullest form. Our background, experiences, age, and attitude; where we have been, what we have seen, and the experiences we have had—all have a great bearing on the degree to which each one of us develops our innate capacity for creativity.

From an early age, we are taught to conform. Even as children, we feel a great need to be accepted by others, to not only be liked by, but to be like others. If left unchallenged, this deeply ingrained habit of conformity may last a lifetime, becoming a major stumbling block to our creative drive and artistic expression. No one wants to be distinguished by mistakes and stupidity, and so we are afraid to attempt anything new and different because we fear failure. Do not be afraid to fail; if one never fails for a lack of trying, this in itself is the ultimate failure!

Choose instead to be creative. It will require determination, perseverance, observation, and flexibility, but it is well worth the effort. Every artist was at one time a beginner, whether his or her art was painting, sculpting, or floral design. Artists do not become highly skilled by watching someone else paint and wistfully wishing they could paint as well. It is only by practice that a high level of skill is reached, and even overreached, time and again; creativity in any field is a continual evolution, the result of hard work as we learn only by doing, over and over.

At one time it was believed that an individual was either creative or not—and that if not, nothing could be done to develop creativity. There has been a rethinking on this matter, however, in light of recent studies that have proven creativity is a skill that can be strengthened like any other. Research by Professor Roger W. Sperry indicates that the two sides of the human brain process information in vastly different ways. Verbal, logical reasoning is controlled by the left side of the brain; creative, perceptual thinking is a function of the right side of the brain. Dr. Betty Edwards has taken this research a step further in her book, *Drawing on the Right Side of the Brain,* in which she tells the reader how to change from one mode of thinking to the other. Obviously, the creative flower arranger ought to be tuned in to the right side of the brain, and with workbook-like exercises, her book explains how to do just that.

Creativity is not limited to artistic ventures; we all face opportunities to use our creative abilities on a daily basis. Deciding what to wear, adding our own touch to a recipe, decorating a room, or even rearranging the accent pieces on a mantel: each can be a creative undertaking—or each can be a repeat of the way we have always done it. Many a missed opportunity for creativity can be attributed to the spirit—or lack of it—behind these few words. "The way we have always done it," though perhaps fresh at first try, quickly becomes tedious, dull, and boring!

Obstacles to creativity come in many forms, ranging from the serious to the trivial, and are often self-imposed. We defeat ourselves at the outset when we try to do too many things at one time or copy thoughtlessly the work of others. Perhaps the most insidious undermining is in the self-defeating attitude we adopt. If one thinks "I'm not very creative" or "This won't work," the arrangement is doomed from the start. Develop a positive, open, relaxed attitude; remind yourself that you, too, are a creative individual.

Creativity is nothing more than putting our native creative abilities into action. A creative individual comes to thrive on challenges, adventures, and new ideas; one is not "stretched" creatively by sticking to comfortable old ways and old combinations. There is a descriptive phrase for this: it is called "being in a rut." Be flexible, willing to change, and, above all, enthusiastic at the prospect. Have the courage to do something different; never fear doing something "wrong." Be willing to take risks. Ask yourself, "What is the worst that can happen?" Tune out criticism; it is only one person's opinion and may have been offered for the wrong reason, perhaps only to hurt rather than to help.

Floral design is a transitory visual language, making visible creatively that which we cannot describe in words, a singular reflection of the artist's innermost being. In Creative floral designs, the arranger reconstructs the building blocks of geometric form—cubes, spheres, cones, and cylinders—into new relationships of verticals, horizontals, diagonals, and patterns. We are challenged to see the same shapes again, in new form. Successful creative work is not a repetition of what we have already done or what someone else has done. Admittedly, nothing is totally new, but by adding our own vision and insight, the result is our own creative concept.

Flexibility is a major requirement of the creative mind. We must resist the urge to repeat the same old thing, even if it has worked in the past. Venture into the unknown; be inventive and daring each time you are faced with an opportunity for design. Begin with a concept, an idea, your own feelings about a subject. Using the elements and principles of design, add your own craftsmanship to illustrate a concept. As a floral designer, one must expect to pick and choose, accept and reject, arrange and rearrange.

As you explore your way into the creation of a new concept, exercise artistic license. Superimpose one form over another. Use your imagination. Ask yourself "What if?" as each new component is introduced. What if this container were to be used with different line material? Or if this line were to go in the opposite direction? Or these colors combined?

Do the unexpected. Incorporate a beautiful piece of decorative wood in a new manner. Mount it on a rod, use it in a different container, place it on its side, or upside down. Suspend it and use the resulting form instead of a container. Place it within an open frame.

Creative designs often use very ordinary components; exotic materials are not a necessity. It is more striking—and more of an exercise of our creativity—to use commonplace materials in uncommon ways. As we have said, garden-grown plant material, with its wider range of developmental stages and sizes, is as good or better than what we can typically purchase from the florist.

This Creative design, previously paired with a Collage, is equally effective alone. The dramatic form created by the massing of iris on the right is balanced by the round, textured form of palm on the left. Adding further interest, the color and rougher texture of the palm blends well with the textured portion of the container, while the texture of the iris repeats the container's smoother portions.

In Creative design, frames are often a vital component, not merely a method of staging. Remove the frame here, and there would be no design—a good test of whether or not a frame has been truly incorporated. Note the pleasing contrast of color between the frame and the manzanita branch.

In this design, the abstract form of decorative wood has been attached inside the frame and painted to match it. Again, the frame is essential to the design. Lilies and clipped fatsia leaves create interest and move the eye through the design.

Two focal areas and two points of emergence qualify this design as Creative. Crumpled metal roofing was sprayed with aluminum paint, overpainted with metallic bronze, and mounted on a metal rod. The resulting form is combined with lilies and thin, blue plastic rods, carefully looped, taped together, and attached at the back. A blue fan and more orange lilies in complementary color harmony comprise a separate and equally strong focal area at bottom.

We tend to look at things without really seeing them, and herein lies the challenge to our creativity. Many mundane objects take on new qualities when combined with other components in a floral design. Isolate an object you would never otherwise think of using; weigh it strictly for its design potential. Analyze its color, form, pattern, and texture, and consider what these characteristics would bring to a design. Keep good taste in mind, however; some items are simply not suitable in floral designs.

Exaggerate line length or height. Stack containers or use multiple containers in a single design, even if they do not match one another. Try different combinations of color, form, and pattern. Make use of distorted or discordant components.

Several frames may be used together; paint them to match the color of one of the other design components. The entire frame may be painted or only the most narrow dimension, creating a colored border around the design. Construct a round or diamond-shaped frame, or one with a built-in square. Experiment with different patterns of stacking with open columns, and create your design using the most effective combination. For a flower show, glue paper or plastic plates, napkins, and glasses to a panel for a Type II Exhibition table.

Question yourself at every step of the design process to be sure you are considering all the possibilities. Before you place the first line in a container, challenge yourself by asking whether or not this is the best container for the design. Is it the best choice of line material? The best, most exciting color combination, or simply the one you have used most recently? Can the line go in another direction? Would different flowers better portray your idea?

When working on an abstract concept, remember that abstraction reveals the essence or essential nature of materials. Avoid a literal image, but rather stylize it; eliminate the literal and emphasize the intangible. Use distortion and exaggeration. Work from your realistic image and simplify it until only the essentials remain. Remember as you pare away that nonobjective Abstract designs do not tell a story; they are purely designs for design's sake.

In flower show work, as we have said, the designer must abide by the requirements of the schedule and the policies of the sponsoring organization. The schedule writers themselves still struggle to strike a happy medium between too many inflexible rules and too few guidelines. In the 1950s and early 1960s, for example, schedules often required "a crescent design of red roses and pine in a black compote." With so many constraints on creativity, is it any wonder that all the designs were woefully similar? "Roses Are Red, My Love" would be a more likely title today, indicating that roses were expected but leaving other details to the designer's creative choice. It is quite enough of a limitation to ask for a specific type of design; schedule writers now often include a few classes that ask merely for a Creative design, allowing the arranger complete freedom to create something unique and beautiful, and better inspiring a pleasingly varied selection of exhibits.

Open your mind to the creative process, and creativity will follow. Use your freedom to explore thoroughly every avenue of choice a design allows. If you are trying something new, try it with conviction. Question yourself as you create, but continue especially to question yourself when faced with the final result. Critiquing your own designs honestly is a crucial step. Begin by deciding what you like best about your design, then go on to look for improvements that might be made. Have the elements been used according to the principles of design?

A piece of frayed tire, found on the shoulder of a freeway, creates a unique form in this Creative design. Two anthuriums and looped ti leaves have been placed to balance the visual weight of the black form.

Would the removal or inclusion of some element improve the design? If for a flower show, does the design conform to the schedule requirements? Is it well balanced, actually and visually? Is there pleasing color balance, color pattern, and textural contrast? Both dominance and contrast of elements? Is there a rhythmic flow throughout the design, or is it static? Are there proper and pleasing proportions of areas and amounts? Is the design properly proportioned in relation to its placement? Are all components in scale with one another? Has space been well used? Does the line material lead the eye through the design in the manner intended? Is lighting suitable? Will the design not only be clearly visible, but also enhanced by the lighting and placement? Is there depth of form? Be patient with yourself. Do not expect every design to be successful early in the learning process—or even much later. Some concepts work well, others do not. You can do nothing better than to learn from each new experience.

Study groups may be very beneficial in this regard. By creating new opportunities for expression, they may be a tremendous help in the development of one's individual creativity, but only if each member feels free to make constructive comments and each recipient takes these comments in the helpful spirit in which they are offered, as something to be considered and studied. Only through open, honest discussion will anything of value result. Such study groups or arrangers' guilds will be most effective if membership is limited to a maximum of twelve individuals; break into smaller groups, or start another, rather than allow the group to become unwieldy in size.

The same design with one more anthurium added, providing a strong focal area. Traditionalists will find this design more appealing than the first version.

Beginners should focus on Traditional Early 20th-Century American designs. As we have tried to emphasize, they are basic to flower arranging and must be thoroughly mastered before one may safely move on to Creative designs. One needs first to know what the basic rules are before learning how and when those rules may be successfully broken or ignored! For those more experienced, the following Creative study exercises may be included as given in lesson plans or taken as inspiration for further thought.

One lesson is most interesting as a means of highlighting the differences in individual work. Obtain a number of identical, inexpensive containers from a wholesale house or similar source, one for each member. The group leader or appointed individual supplies in amounts suitable for the class size two or three different sorts of line materials, foliage, and flowers. Members choose from this common store plant and line material for use in their individual designs. They should come to the meeting prepared with their own needleholder, floral clay, and/or oasis. Set a time limit for the creation of the arrangements, and have a discussion of the results. There will undoubtedly be a wide variation of styles, and therefore a lively exchange of ideas.

Another worthwhile exercise—sure to provide new ideas for use of containers—is for each member to bring a container from home to the meeting. Number the containers and have members draw for them. The program chairman alone may provide the plant material or each member may have been asked to bring some line, foliage, and flowers to make up a supply for the class, from which

Some expect designs using vegetables and flowers to be dull, not to say Traditional. Not so! In this Creative design, clipped zebra grass provides a strong framework of vertical line, reinforced by fresh asparagus spears. Clipped, variegated foliage combines well with creamy anthuriums, and the whole is balanced by the single large artichoke on the right.

everyone picks and chooses materials for inclusion in their designs. Again, set a specific time period to work on the designs, and critique the results. Members then take their own container home, along with the design that has been created in it by a fellow classmember, to study it further at their leisure.

It is always useful to bring in someone not of the group to critique the designs. Suggestions should be offered only in the most helpful spirit, and members must be able to take this constructive criticism in the manner in which it is intended. You may not always agree with the other person's opinion, but that opinion should always be considered. This is how we learn: not by the absolute, undebated acceptance of another's opinion, but by its due consideration.

Other ideas for assignments will invariably occur to the membership or the program chairman. Besides the challenge of arranging any Creative design type discussed in chapter eight or table setting discussed in chapter nine, the program chairman might choose as a study topic the same design with certain strictures specified, including

- An Abstract design using only natural materials.
- An Abstract design of fruits and/or vegetables with foliage permitted.
- An Abstract design using only foliage.
- An Assemblage combining five different, unrelated components.
- A Botanical design featuring fruits and/or vegetables.
- A Creative design in two nonidentical containers.
- A Creative design using man-made material for line.
- A Creative design in a contrived container.
- A Type I Exhibition table, using two or more frames.
- A Type I Exhibition table, staged on a kitchen stool.
- A Type II Exhibition table, staged on a panel.
- A Type II Exhibition table, staged on the floor.
- A Type II Exhibition table, staged in a basket.

Whatever the assignment, it is an absolute necessity that each member come prepared to every meeting with a design to be critiqued. Regularly scheduled meetings assure practice—and practice is essential for creative development.

In addition to work in a design study group, expand your horizons by visiting art galleries, flower shows, and museums. Read art books and magazines, as well as interior design publications. Check the local florist shops to see what is happening in the professional area. Before beginning a design, do a sketch of it; simple lines, circles, and oblongs can indicate the elements. At this early stage, doodling can be quite productive and a real aid to the creative process. Look up definitions of unfamiliar terms used in the schedule if you intend your design for a flower show. Use both National Council's *Handbook* glossary and even a dictionary if necessary until you are satisfied that you understand the meaning of every word.

Never feel that your work must equal or in some way come up to that of another individual. You are an individual, and your designs will be best when they reflect that individuality. Copying the work of others is not creative; by imitating, we most certainly are not expressing our own reactions to a subject. It is seldom that we can recreate even our own designs, if they were a true welling-up of creativity to begin with. Respect the work of others, but remember that we all develop our own unique style; this is as it should be. The work of other arrangers is good for the purposes of developing our own innate creativity only insofar as it ignites ideas and gets the creative juices flowing.

The designs in this book are intended only to illustrate my own personal style and to serve as a springboard from which readers, I hope, will develop a style all their own. If you have studied the photographs carefully, you can easily identify that pervading style: a preference for line and few plant materials. Given time and practice, you too will develop and identify your own unique, inimitable style.

You are a creative individual—believe it!

A Creative design, with ginger blooms featured in two points of emergence. The red-edged foliage has been hot-glued directly to the container, creating interesting planes which echo its lines and form.

Loops of black vine repeat the lines of the metal sculpture in this Creative design. The bright yellow lilies appear lustrous, contrasting dramatically with the black form and blue background. No mechanic detracts from the effect: a black cupholder is used at bottom, and the water pick that serves the upper grouping of plant material has been covered with black electrician's tape.

Different designers, given the same container and line material, will invariably create their own personal interpretation. Here, a visually heavy container is combined with strong lines of wisteria vine and lilies in an unusual Abstract arrangement. Design by Deen Day Smith.

The same container and line material are now arranged with birds-of-paradise in an entirely different, equally expressivë Creative design.

Two pieces of decorative wood combine with pincushion protea to successfully balance a visually heavy container in this Creative design. Clipped foliage adds strength and contrast.

A far more interesting variant has been created by ignoring the usual method of determining line material's height in relation to the container. With the uppermost piece of wood removed, the remaining decorative wood and the placement of plant material together more obviously echo the form of the container.

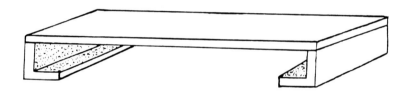

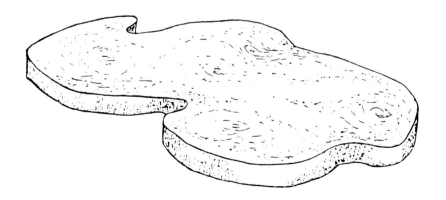

APPENDIX

Dimensions: A Closer Look at Staging Methods

BASES

Illustrated here are three common examples of bases that may be used under a flower arrangement; some will be most suitable for use with a particular sort of design. For instance, the scroll-like base pictured at top has an Oriental flavor and will assist in the interpretation of a design in the Oriental manner. Next is a more modern base whose clean, straight lines would be especially appropriate in Creative work. An inexpensive version of either of these bases is easily constructed, requiring only minimal woodworking skills along with wood trims and quarter-inch plywood scraps from the local lumberyard. The trim pieces can be drilled and attached with small nails or glue. If you are nailing the pieces together, countersink the nails and cover the nail heads with putty. Let dry. Sand the area smooth and paint the entire piece with several coats of the desired color. Remember that matte or semi-gloss paint is a better, more natural complement for most flower arrangements than a high gloss.

For a more free-form effect, the last base shown, made from a thin slice of wood cut from a tree stump or log, would be most appropriate. A landscaping or firewood business often has such pieces in stock, and the slice will already have been successfully dried without splitting. Bases may also be had from florist, hobby, specialty, or craft shops, or at garage and estate sales. As discussed in chapter three, weathered barn boards or decorative wood are other possibilities. Keep your eyes open; you may even create a base of your own design!

BACKGROUNDS

Backgrounds are typically one-sided with a flat extension attached at the bottom and extended on only one side. Backgrounds can be made in any size, of course, but as they are primarily used in flower show work, the required dimensions are usually indicated in the schedule. As a helpful, logical courtesy to participants, most local flower show committees decide upon standard dimensions to be used at all shows. Backgrounds may be provided by the flower show committee or the exhibitor. If it falls to the designer, the challenge will be to make them stand in an upright, stable position, so a rigid material is a must. Many backgrounds are like the one pictured here: constructed of quarter-inch plywood, pressed wood, or particle board, with the bottom extension permanently attached. The bottom extension can be forward of the background with the design placed on it, or it may simply be a stabilizing element, turned to the back and clamped to the edge of the table. An alternate uses no extension and is made to stand by using two short lengths of two-by-four lumber with slots cut for the insertion of the background. The "feet" must be long enough for the background to be stable, but short enough to remain unobtrusive. Backgrounds are usually covered with solid-colored fabric or painted in a hue, complementary to the design. They must be stored flat to avoid warping.

Backgrounds are falling out of favor in flower show work; many shows are requiring frames, open columns, and the other staging methods which follow in their stead.

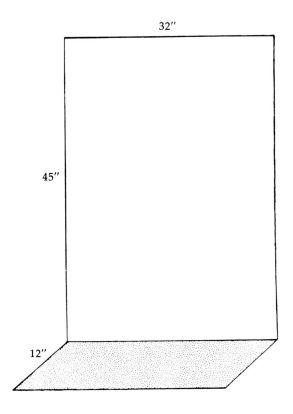

BOXES

Boxes may be incorporated into the flower arrangement itself or used as a method of staging designs or Exhibition table settings. The creative arranger will find many uses for these versatile items, which can be easily made in graduated sizes by one with even minimal carpentry skills. Choose one-by-six or one-by-four lumber which will yield boards approximately five-and-one-half or three-and-one-half inches in width, respectively. Boxes of any dimension may be used, but those illustrated here are found by many to be the most useful. Nail the boards together, being careful to keep the corners square. Countersink the nails, cover with putty, and let dry. Sand smooth and apply several coats of paint.

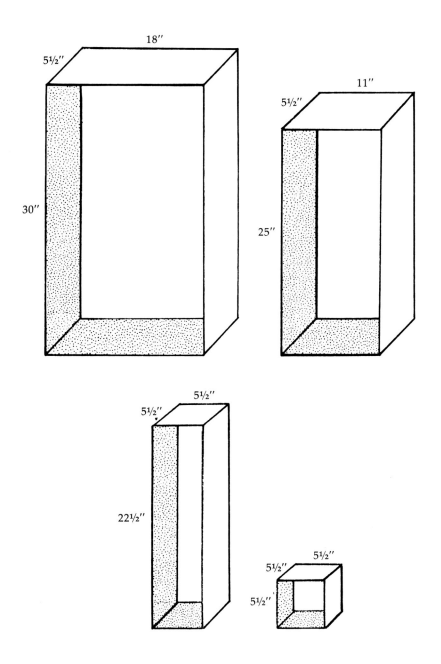

FRAMES

Frames, whether used singly or in pairs, are a lovely way to add dimension to an arrangement. They may be made in any size, but the ones given in the accompanying illustrations have proven most useful. If one possesses the first two sizes and one with the dimensions of the footed frame, the three may be used in many combinations. When making multiple frames, always cut an extra square of the board; painted the same color as the frame, it can be used to level a frame placed crossways inside another. In addition to their versatility, frames in assorted sizes can be stacked inside one another for storage or transportation.

Use a carpenter's square to make sure corners are perfect as the frame is constructed. Metal corner braces should be positioned on the back side of the frame to retain the perfect corners and straight sides. Countersink the nails and cover with putty. Let dry. Sand smooth and paint. Remember that for these and all staging items, color can be speedily changed with a fresh coat of paint.

Once constructed, any size frame can be made more stable for use with a Hanging design or other suspended parts by attaching, permanently or temporarily, two pieces of two-by-four lumber for "feet." They should be about two inches longer than the depth of the frame for stability. To suspend the design or other elements from the frame, one or more small, screw-in hooks can be attached to the inside top of the frame and painted to match it. The hook can be removed when necessary and if it was a properly small one, the hole it leaves will not be noticeable.

Creative arrangers may design and construct frames in other shapes to add creative touches to their work, but a frame shaped like a diamond is best made by an experienced carpenter. The angles are difficult and great patience is necessary, though beyond this, it is joined together and finished off like any other frame. The dimensions suggested here make a diamond frame large enough for a Hanging design.

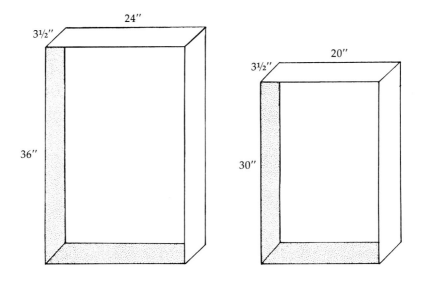

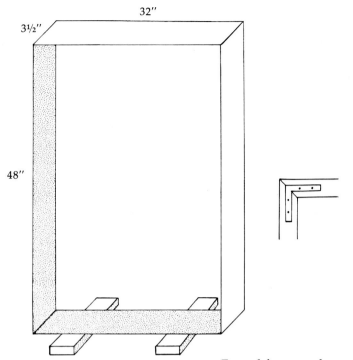

Footed frame and corner brace

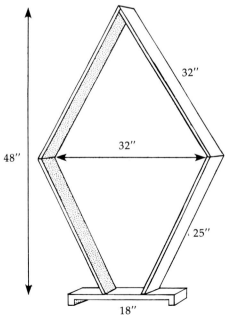

Diamond frame

NICHES

Niches are easily made by anyone who can wield an all-purpose utility knife and apply tape. If they are made from commercial art foam, they are not only simple to construct, but light in weight and easy to handle. Using a sharp utility knife, cut the art foam along a straight edge, such as a carpenter's square or a straight board. On a flat surface, place the pieces meant for the wings, or side panels, on either side of the center panel, leaving a quarter inch of space between each piece: if no gap is left, the niche cannot be folded. Be sure the edges are straight. Using one-sided, white carpet tape, tape over the center of one gap, attaching the wing to the center panel. Turn the two boards over and tape on the back side of the seam as well. Repeat the process to attach the second side panel on the opposite side of the center panel. Finish with paint or fabric. The wings of a niche may be folded in either direction: forward or back, or one in each direction, as pictured. Niches must be folded and stored flat to prevent warping. Never place heavy objects on a folded niche as the foam is easily damaged.

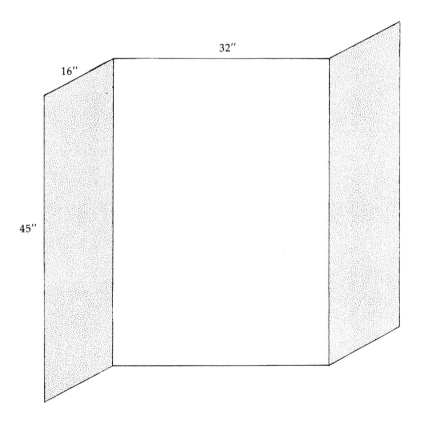

OPEN COLUMNS

Though open columns are most often used to support a Creative design, they may be incorporated into large designs or used to stage multiple coordinated designs. Again, having a collection of columns of various dimensions which can be combined in different ways adds to their versatility and makes transportation and storage a breeze because they can be nested. Remember that despite their name, open columns—like boxes and other staging methods—may be used horizontally as well as vertically in a design. Open columns are constructed in the same way as frames and boxes: countersink the nails, cover nail heads with putty, let dry, sand, and paint the desired color.

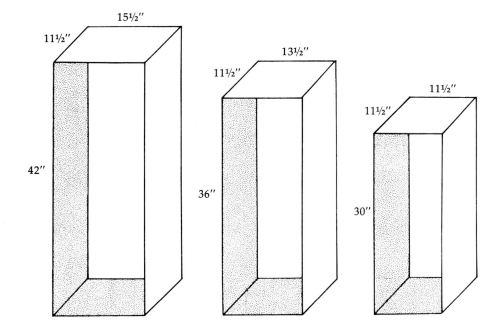

For Further Reading

Aaronson, Marian. 1979. *Design With Plant Material*. 2nd ed. Fakenham, Norfolk, United Kingdom: Sharp Print Management.

_____. 1980. *The Art of Flower Arranging*. 4th ed. Whitestable, Kent, United Kingdom: Whitestable Litho.

_____. 1981. *Flowers in the Modern Manner*. Fakenham, Norfolk, United Kingdom: Sharp Print Management.

Ascher, Amalie Adler. 1974. *The Complete Flower Arranger*. New York: Simon & Schuster.

Berrall, Julia S. 1951. *Flowers and Table Settings*. London: Studio Publications; New York: Thomas Y. Crowell Co.

_____. 1953. *A History of Flower Arrangement*. London: Studio Publications; New York: Thomas Y. Crowell Co.

Birren, Faber. 1961. *Creative Color*. New York: Van Nostrand Reinhold.

Brack, Edith. 1982. *Modern Flower Arranging*. London: B. T. Batsford.

Brandenburger, Nelda H. 1969. *Interpretive Flower Arrangement*. New York: Hearthside Press.

Brigadier, Anne. 1970. *Collage: A Complete Guide for Artists*. New York: Watson-Guptill Publications.

Clements, Julia. 1981. *The Art of Arranging a Flower*. New York: Walker Publishing Co.

Coe, Stella. 1988. *Ikebana*. 2nd ed. Ed. Mary L. Stewart. New York: Gallery Books and W. H. Smith Publishers.

Cyphers, Emma Hodkinson. 1958. *Design and Depth in Flower Arrangement*. New York: Hearthside Press.

_____. 1959. *Modern Art in Flower Arrangement*. New York: Hearthside Press.

_____. 1963. *Nature, Art and Flower Arrangement*. New York: Hearthside Press.

_____. 1964. *Modern Abstract Flower Arrangement*. New York: Hearthside Press.

De Grandis, Luigina. 1986. *Theory and Use of Color*. 2nd ed. New York: Harry N. Abrams.

Edwards, Betty. 1989. *Drawing on the Right Side of the Brain*. 2nd ed. Los Angeles: Jeremy P. Tarcher.

Edwards, David. 1979. *How to be More Creative*. Campbell, CA: Occasional Productions.

Hailstone, Pamela. 1979. *Modern Design in Floral Art*. Auckland, New Zealand: Jacaranda Press.

Hamel, Esther Veramae. 1982. *The Encyclopedia of Judging and Exhibiting*. 5th ed. St. Ignatius, MT: Ponderosa Publishers.

Hannay, Frances J. 1948. *Period Flower Arrangements*. St. Louis, MO: National Council of State Garden Clubs.

Hirsch, Sylvia. 1962. *The Art of Table Setting and Flower Arrangement*. New York: Thomas Y. Crowell Co.

_____ . 1987. *The Art of Judging and Exhibiting Flower Arrangements*. 2nd ed. New York. Privately published.

Joosten, Titia. 1988. *Flower Drying with a Microwave*. Trans. Marianne Weigman. Asheville, NC: Lark Books. First published in the Netherlands in 1985.

Knight, Mary. 1965. *Abstract and Not-so-Abstract Flower Arrangements*. Princeton, NJ: D. Van Nostrand Co.

Leland, Nita. 1990. *The Creative Artist*. Cincinnati, OH: North Light Books and Writer's Digest Books.

Marchesseau, Danielle. 1989. *The Intimate World of Alexander Calder*. Paris: Solange Thierry.

Mayer, Ralph. 1969. *A Dictionary of Art Terms and Techniques*. New York: Thomas Y. Crowell Co.

Mitchell, Peter. 1973. *Great Flower Painters: Four Centuries of Floral Art*. Woodstock, NY: Overlook Press.

National Council of State Garden Clubs, Inc. 1987. *Handbook for Flower Shows*. Rev. ed. St. Louis, MO: National Council of State Garden Clubs.

Reister, Dorothy W. 1971. *Design for Flower Arrangers*. 2nd ed. Princeton, NJ: D. Van Nostrand Co.

Sparnon, Norman. 1979. *A Guide to Japanese Flower Arrangement*. Tokyo: Shufunotomo Co.

_____ . 1982. *Creative Japanese Flower Arrangement*. Tokyo: Shufunotomo Co.

Stangos, Nikos. ed. 1981. *Concepts of Modern Art*. 2nd ed. New York: Harper & Row.

Sutter, Anne Bernat. 1983. *A New Approach to Design Principles*. 3rd ed. Overland, MO: Sutter Publishing Co.

Teshigahara, Kasumi. 1980. *Kasumi's Ikebana for All Seasons*. Tokyo: Shufunotomo Co.

Thomas, Robert C. 1986– . Guidelines. American Guild of Flower Arrangers. A semi-annual publication, it is the official bulletin of the guild.

Webb, Iris, ed. 1979. *The Complete Guide to Flower and Foliage Arrangement*. Garden City, NY: Doubleday and Co.

Wilson, Helen Van Pelt. 1971. *Flowers, Space and Motion*. New York: Simon & Schuster.

Wong, Wucius. 1987. *Principles of Color Design*. New York: Van Nostrand Reinhold.

Index

Numbers in **bold** refer to pages with related illustrations or photographs.